Congressional
Research
Service

Oil Sands and the Keystone XL Pipeline: Background and Selected Environmental Issues

Jonathan L. Ramseur, Coordinator
Specialist in Environmental Policy

Richard K. Lattanzio
Analyst in Environmental Policy

Linda Luther
Analyst in Environmental Policy

Paul W. Parfomak
Specialist in Energy and Infrastructure Policy

Nicole T. Carter
Specialist in Natural Resources Policy

July 16, 2012

Congressional Research Service

7-5700

www.crs.gov

R42611

CRS Report for Congress

Prepared for Members and Committees of Congress

Summary

If constructed, the Keystone XL pipeline would transport crude oil (e.g., synthetic crude oil or diluted bitumen) derived from oil sands in Alberta, Canada to destinations in the United States. Because the pipeline crosses an international border, it requires a Presidential Permit that is issued by the Department of State (DOS). The permit decision rests on a "national interest" determination, a term not defined in the authorizing Executive Orders. DOS states that it has "significant discretion" in the factors it examines in this determination. Key events related to the Presidential Permit include:

- **September 19, 2008**: TransCanada submitted an application for a Presidential Permit for its Keystone XL pipeline.

- **November 10, 2011**: DOS announced it needed additional information concerning alternative pipeline routes through the Nebraska Sandhills.

- **January 18, 2012**: In response to a legislative mandate in P.L. 112-78, DOS, with the President's consent, announced its denial of the Keystone XL permit.

- **May 4, 2012**: TransCanada submitted a revised permit application to DOS.

Although some groups have opposed previous oil pipeline permits, opposition to the Keystone XL proposal has generated substantially more interest among environmental stakeholders. Pipeline opponents are not a monolithic group: some raise concerns about potential local impacts, such as oil spills or extraction impacts in Canada; some argue the pipeline would have national energy and climate change policy implications.

A number of key studies indicate that oil sands crude has a higher greenhouse gas (GHG) emissions intensity than many other forms of crude oil. The primary reason for the higher intensity: oil sands are heavy oils with a high viscosity, requiring more energy- and resource-intensive activities to extract. However, analytical results vary due to different modeling assumptions. Moreover, industry stakeholders point out that many analyses indicate that GHG emissions from oil sands crude oil are comparable to other heavy crudes, some of which are produced and/or consumed in the United States.

Because of oil sands' increased emissions intensity, further oil sands development runs counter to some stakeholders' energy and climate change policy objectives. These objectives may vary based on differing views concerning the severity of climate change risk and/or the need for significant mitigation efforts. Opponents worry that oil sands crude oil will account for a greater percentage of U.S. oil consumption over time, making GHG emissions reduction more difficult. On the other hand, neither issuance of a Presidential Permit nor increased oil sands development would preclude the implementation of energy/climate policies that would support less carbon intensive fuels or energy efficiency improvements.

A primary local/regional environmental concern of any oil pipeline is the risk of a spill. Environmental groups have argued that both the pipeline's operating parameters and the material being transported imposes an increased risk of spill. Industry stakeholders have been critical of these assertions. To examine the concerns, Congress included provisions in P.L. 112-90 requiring a review of current oil pipeline regulations and a risk analysis of oil sands crude.

Opponents of the Keystone XL pipeline and oil sands development often highlight the environmental impacts that pertain to the region in which the oil sands resources are extracted. Potential impacts include, among others, land disturbance and water resource issues. In general, these local/regional impacts from Canadian oil sands development may not directly affect public health or the environment in the United States. Within the context of a Presidential Permit, the mechanism to consider local Canadian impacts is unclear.

Contents

Figures

Tables

Appendixes

Contacts

Introduction

The proposed Keystone XL pipeline has received considerable attention in recent months. If constructed, the pipeline would transport crude oil (e.g., synthetic crude oil or diluted bitumen) derived from oil sands in Alberta, Canada to destinations in the United States and ultimately the international market. Policymakers continue to debate various issues associated with the proposed pipeline. Although some groups have opposed previous oil pipelines—Alberta Clipper and the Keystone mainline, both of which are operating—opposition to the Keystone XL proposal has generated substantially more interest among environmental stakeholders.

Before the Keystone XL pipeline can be constructed, its owner/operator, TransCanada,[1] must receive a Presidential Permit, which is issued by the State Department. The decision to issue this permit has provided (and continues to provide) a rallying point for environmental groups.

The Presidential Permit application—submitted by TransCanada—for the pipeline's construction represents a singular decision made by the Administration that the pipeline would serve the national interest. Such a decision requires the identification of factors that would inform that determination, as well as resulting impacts. For environmental groups opposed to the project, the identification of specific environmental impacts associated with the project provides evidence on which arguments against the project may be based.

Pipeline opponents are not a monolithic group and their concerns vary. Some raise concerns about potential local impacts, such as oil spills. Some highlight the oil extraction impacts in Canada. Some argue the pipeline would have national energy and climate change policy implications.[2] For these particular opponents, the Presidential Permit decision has been seen as a gauge of the Administration's support for reducing domestic fossil fuel use and greenhouse gas emissions. Thus, the pipeline proposal has provided a vehicle to galvanize advocates interested in climate change mitigation, particularly the reduction or replacement of fossil fuel use.

This report focuses on *selected environmental* concerns raised in conjunction with the proposed pipeline and the oil sands crude it will transport. As such, the environmental issues discussed in this report do not represent an exhaustive list of concerns raised by environmental groups. Moreover, many of the environmental concerns are not unique to oil sands. One could compose analogous lists for all forms of energy: coal, natural gas, nuclear, biofuels, conventional crude oil. Therefore, the oil sands/pipeline issues discussed in this report, when practicable, will be compared to other energy sources, particularly conventional crude oil development.

- **Section One** provides an overview of oil sands by addressing the following questions: what are oil sands; how are they extracted; how do oil sands crude oils compare to other crude oils?

---

[1] TransCanada is a public energy company, based in Canada, that owns oil and natural gas pipelines and power plants, among other assets, in Canada, the United States, and Mexico. See http://www.transcanada.com.

[2] Arguments supporting the pipeline's construction cover an analogous range, from local job creation to national energy security. See CRS Report R41668, *Keystone XL Pipeline Project Key Issues*, by Paul W. Parfomak, Linda Luther, and Adam Vann.

- **Section Two** provides an overview of the Keystone XL pipeline, including a project description; a discussion of the federal requirements to consider environmental impacts from the pipeline, including the Department of State's national interest determination, obligations pursuant to the National Environmental Policy Act, and a list of recent milestones in the national interest determination process; and information about other international oil pipelines.

- **Section Three** discusses selected environmental issues, including greenhouse gas emissions intensity, broader energy policy concerns, pipeline oil spill risks, and two oil sands extraction concerns: land disturbance and water resources.

- An **Appendix** contains additional information.

This report is intended to supplement other CRS reports that address different aspects of the Keystone XL proposal, including:

- CRS Report R41668, *Keystone XL Pipeline Project: Key Issues*, by Paul W. Parfomak, Linda Luther, and Adam Vann.

- CRS Report R42124, *Proposed Keystone XL Pipeline: Legal Issues*, by Adam Vann et al..

- CRS Report R42537, *Canadian Oil Sands: Life-Cycle Assessments of Greenhouse Gas Emissions*, by Richard K. Lattanzio.

Section 1: Oil Sands—Overview

The term oil sands generally refers to a mixture of sand, clay and other minerals, water, and bitumen. Oil sands bitumen is very dense[3] and highly viscous (i.e., resistant to flow). At room temperature, oil sands bitumen has the consistency of cold molasses. This property makes it difficult to transport.[4]

Bitumen can also be processed into a fuel, because it is a form of crude oil that has undergone degradation over geologic time. At some point, the bitumen may have been lighter crude oil that lost its lighter, more volatile components due to natural processes.

---

[3] Oil sands bitumen contains up to 50% (by weight) asphaltenes, a class of hydrocarbon of high molecular weight.

[4] This same property lends itself well to making asphalt—a mixture of asphaltenes and petrolenes—useful for road paving.

"Oil Sands" vs. "Tar Sands"

Oil sands are sometimes described as tar sands, because both the bitumen in oil sands and tar are black and sticky. The term "tar" also refers to a man-made material, generated as a by-product of heating coal to extremely high temperatures, often during gas and coke production. In contrast, bitumen is a naturally occurring substance.

The U.S. Geological Survey states that tar sands is a "generic term that has been used for several decades to describe petroleum-bearing rocks exposed on the Earth's surface."[5] Although some federal government resources refer to the deposits as tar sands,[6] the term seems to be most applied by opponents of oil sands development, as it arguably carries a negative connotation.

Companies developing oil sands reserves must partially process or dilute the bitumen before it can be transported. This processed/diluted bitumen falls into three general categories:

- **Upgraded bitumen, or synthetic crude oil (SCO).** SCO is produced from bitumen at a refinery that turns the very heavy hydrocarbons into a lighter material.

- **Diluted Bitumen (DilBit).** DilBit is bitumen that is blended with lighter hydrocarbons, typically natural gas condensates, to create a lighter, less viscous, and more easily transportable material. DilBit may be blended as 25% to 30% condensate and 70% to 75% bitumen.

- **Synthetic bitumen (Synbit).** Synbit is typically a combination of bitumen and SCO. Blending the lighter SCO with the heavier bitumen results in a product that more closely resembles conventional crude oil. Typically the ratio is 50% synthetic crude and 50% bitumen, but blends, and their resulting properties, may vary significantly.

Figure 1 illustrates the proportions of crude oil types that Canada has exported to the United States in recent years. The figure indicates that "blended bitumen" exports, which includes both Dilbit and Synbit, have nearly tripled in the past six years. They are also expected to constitute most of the growth in oil sands production in the foreseeable future.[7]

---

[5] U.S. Geological Survey, *Natural Bitumen Resources of the United States*, 2006.

[6] See e.g., U.S. Department of the Interior's Bureau of Land Management, "Oil Shale and Tar Sands Programmatic EIS Information Center," at http://ostseis.anl.gov.

[7] Canadian Association of Petroleum Producers, *Crude Oil Forecast, Markets & Pipelines*, June 2012.

Figure 1. U.S. Imports of Canadian Crude Oil by Type
2005-2011

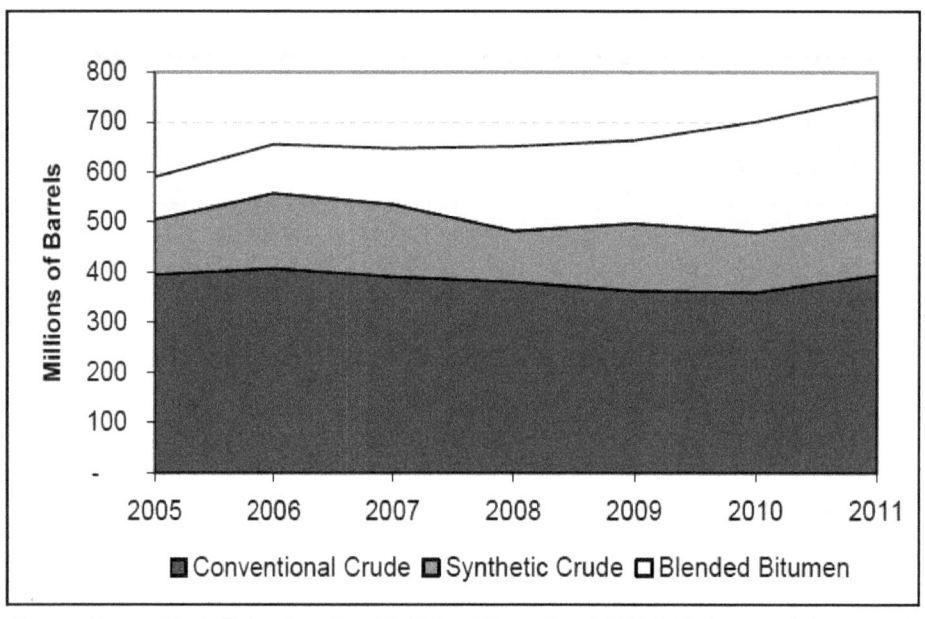

Oil Sands Estimates and Locations

Resource estimates indicate that oil sands deposits are located throughout the world in varying amounts (**Figure 2**). By far, the two largest estimated deposits of oil sands are in Canada, particularly the Province of Alberta,[8] and in Venezuela's Orinoco Oil Belt (**Figure 2**). As stated by the U.S. Geological Survey, the "resource quantities reported here … are intended to suggest, rather than define the resource volumes that could someday be of commercial interest."[9] For a variety of reasons (e.g., technology and economics), only a small percentage—less than 0.4% based on information in 2007—of the estimated oil sands resources are currently being produced.[10]

---

[8] Some oil sands deposits are located in northwest Saskatchewan next to the Alberta deposit, but the resource base has not been officially determined (Canadian Association of Petroleum Producers (CAPP), *Crude Oil Forecast, Markets & Pipelines*, June 2011).

[9] U.S. Geological Survey (USGS), *Heavy Oil and Natural Bitumen Resources in Geological Basins of the World*, 2007.

[10] U.S. Geological Survey (USGS), *Heavy Oil and Natural Bitumen Resources in Geological Basins of the World*, 2007.

Figure 2. Illustration of Estimated In-Place Oil Sands Resources by Region
Billion barrels

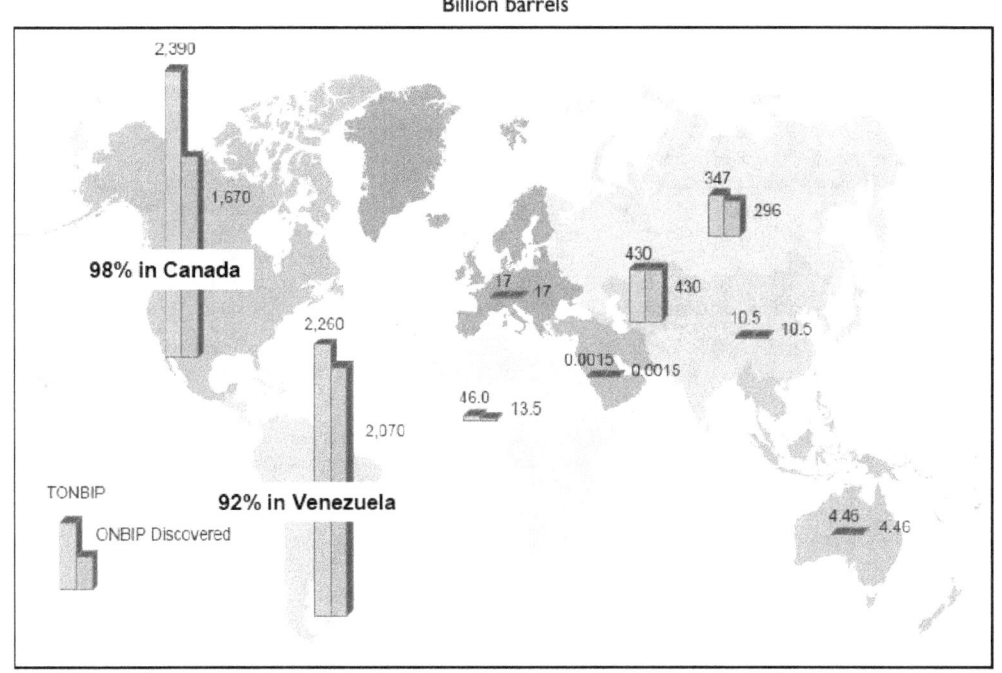

Source: Prepared by CRS; original figure and data from U.S. Geological Survey (USGS), *Heavy Oil and Natural Bitumen Resources in Geological Basins of the World,* 2007. CRS added the notes regarding percentages in Canada and Venezuela, based on the USGS report data.

Notes: Column bars represent "original natural bitumen in place-discovered" (ONBIP Discovered) and "total original natural bitumen in place" (TONBIP). The latter includes ONBIP-discovered plus "prospective additional oil," which is "the amount of resource in an unmeasured section or portion of a known deposit be ieved to be present as a result of inference from geological and often geophysical study." These estimates are substantially higher than "proven reserve" estimates, discussed below. The different regions in the figure include: North America, South America, Europe, Africa, Transcaucasia, Middle East, Russia, South Asia, East Asia, Southeast Asia and Oceania.

Perhaps a more useful estimate of oil resources is "proven reserves." According to the Energy Information Administration (EIA), proven energy reserves are "estimated quantities of energy sources that analysis of geologic and engineering data demonstrates with reasonable certainty are recoverable under existing economic and operating conditions." [11] The Government of Alberta estimates that its proven oil sands reserves are approximately 170 billion barrels, [12] which accounts for 97% of Canada's total proven oil reserves, 7%-10% of the total estimated resource in Canada's geologic basin (**Figure 2**).

---

[11] See EIA Glossary at http://www.eia.gov/.

[12] Government of Alberta, "About the Resource," at http://oilsands.alberta.ca/resource.html (accessed April 6, 2012).

U.S. Oil Sands: Resource Estimates and Extraction Efforts

Estimates of U.S. oil sands deposits vary. According to a "measured-in-place" estimate from the U.S. Geological Survey (USGS), deposits of oil sands in the United States may contain approximately 36 billion barrels.[13] This is not a proven reserve estimate, but an estimate comparable to the "original natural bitumen" estimates in **Figure 2**. As that figure illustrates, the estimated resource of oil sands in the United States accounts for approximately 2% of the total North American oil sands resource.

The estimated resource of U.S. oil sands is located in several states in varying amounts: Alaska (41%), Utah (33%), Texas (11%), Alabama (5%), California (5%), and Kentucky (5%).[14] The deposits are not uniform. For instance, some deposits (estimated at less than 15%)[15] in Utah may be amenable to surface mining techniques. In contrast, the Alaska deposits are buried below several thousand feet of permafrost.[16] In addition, the physical/chemical properties of oil sands can differ by location. The U.S. Bureau of Land Management (BLM) states that "Canadian tar sands are different than U.S. tar sands in that Canadian tar sands are water wetted, while U.S tar sands are hydrocarbon wetted." Such differences may influence whether extraction of particular deposits is economically and technologically viable.

According to BLM, oil from oil sands deposits is not produced on a significant commercial level in the United States.[17] Although prior attempts, dating back decades, have been made in several locations, various challenges hindered commercial development.[18]

A comprehensive assessment of oil sands-related activities in the United States is beyond the scope of this report. Efforts to extract U.S. oil sands continue at several locations, particularly in Utah. A Canadian company, U.S. Oil Sands, owns leases in Utah that cover over 32,000 acres.[19] As of the date of this report, the company is in the process of obtaining required permits to begin relatively small-scale oil sands mining operations on approximately 200 acres of state-owned lands.[20] According to the company, it plans to begin operations in late 2013,[21] achieving an initial output of approximately 2,000 barrels per day.[22] This project has been opposed by environmental groups.[23]

Figure 3 illustrates the estimated proven oil reserves for the top 15 nations in 2011. Canada ranks third behind Venezuela and Saudi Arabia, due to its supply of oil sands in Alberta.[24]

---

[13] See USGS, *Natural Bitumen Resources of the United States*, 2006, at http://pubs.usgs.gov/fs/2006/3133/pdf/FS2006-3133_508.pdf. The USGS estimates are largely based on studies from 1984 and 1995.

[14] The USGS assessment identifies additional states—Oklahoma, New Mexico, and Wyoming—with potential oil sands deposits, but these would each account for less than one percent of the total U.S. estimate.

[15] See Bureau of Land Management, *Draft Programmatic Environmental Impact Statement and Possible Land Use Plan Amendments for Allocation of Oil Shale and Tar Sands Resources on Lands Administered by the Bureau of Land Management in Colorado, Utah, and Wyoming*, Appendix B, January 2012.

[16] V.A. Kamath et al, "Assessment of Resource and Recovery Potential of Ugnu Tar Sands, North Slope Alaska," in Meyer, R.F., ed., Heavy crude and tar sands—Fueling for a clean and safe environment: Sixth United Nations Institute for Training and Research (UNITAR) Conference on Heavy Crude and Tar Sands, Houston, Texas, February 12–17, 1995, p. 141–157.

[17] Bureau of Land Management, Oil Shale and Tar Sands Programmatic EIS Information Center, at http://ostseis.anl.gov.

[18] An archived CRS report includes a history of oil sands activities in the United States. See CRS Report RL34258, *North American Oil Sands History of Development, Prospects for the Future*, by Marc Humphries.

[19] See U.S. Oil Sands website, at http://www.usoilsandsinc.com.

[20] See U.S. Oil Sands, Notice of Intention to Commence Large Mining Operations, 2009; Utah Department of Environmental Quality, Administrative Hearings conducted May 2012, both available at http://www.deq.utah.gov/locations/prsprings/index.htm.

[21] U.S. Oil Sands, Press Release, "US Oil Sands Announces Q1 2012 Financial Results, Provides Operational Update and Grant of Options," at http://www.usoilsandsinc.com/documents/news/USO-2012-05-29-pressrelease.pdf.

[22] U.S. Oil Sands, Notice of Intention to Commence Large Mining Operations, 2009.

[23] See e.g., Utah Tar Sands Resistance, at http://tarsandsutah.blueskyinstitute.org.

[24] EIA "International Energy Statistics," at http://www.eia.gov/.

Figure 3. EIA Estimated Proven Oil Reserves

Top 15 Nations in 2011—Compared to 2001 Estimates

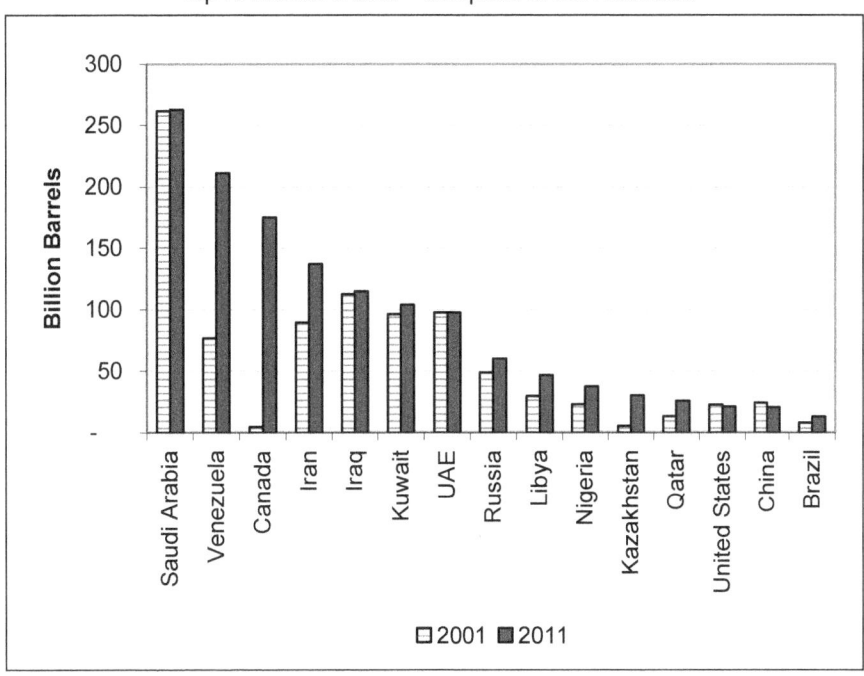

Source: Prepared by CRS; data from EIA, "International Energy Statistics," at http://www.eia.gov/.

Notes: United States' proven reserves for 2011 based on data from 2009, because that is the most recent year of available data.

Proven reserve estimates can change dramatically over a relatively short time (**Figure 3**). EIA data indicate that Canada's proven reserve estimate increased from approximately 5 billion barrels of oil (BBO) in 2002 to 175 BBO in 2003.[25] Similarly, Venezuela's estimated proven reserves increased by more than 100 BBO between 2010 and 2011.[26] The increases resulted from the addition of oil sands in Canada and extra-heavy oil in Venezuela to the total estimated proven reserves for each country.

Oil Sands Extraction Processes

Oil sands extraction processes are generally divided into two categories: mining and in situ operations, which are described below. **Figure 4** identifies the locations of areas accessible to mining and in situ sites of oil sands in Alberta. According to the Government of Alberta, 80% of the Canadian oil sands are accessible by in situ methods only.

---

[25] EIA "International Energy Statistics," at http://www.eia.gov/.

[26] See EIA "International Energy Statistics," at http://www.eia.gov/.

Figure 4. Alberta Oil Sands

Potential Mining and In Situ Sites

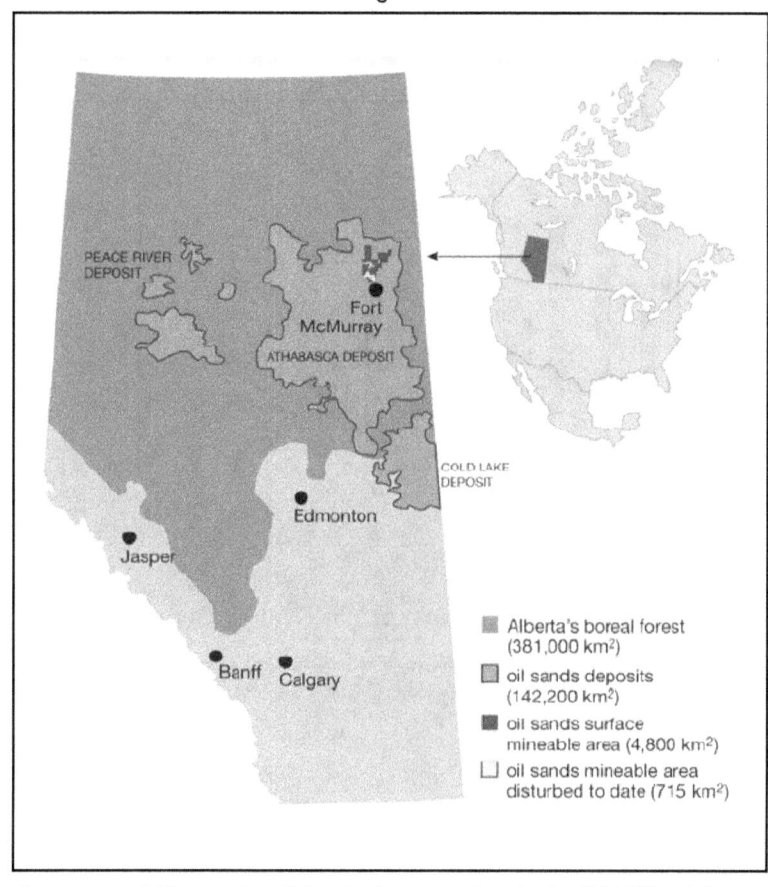

Source: Government of Alberta, at http://oilsands.a berta.ca/reclamation.html#JM-OilSandsArea

Notes: According to the Canadian Association of Petroleum Producers, smaller oil sands deposits are in northwest Saskatchewan next to the Alberta deposit, but the resource base has not been officially determined (*Crude Oil: Forecast, Markets & Pipelines*, June 2011).

Currently, mining operations account for slightly more than 50% of current production. Assuming a business-as-usual scenario, the Canadian Association of Petroleum Producers (CAPP) projects that ratio would remain roughly the same until 2025.[27] However, an oil sands growth scenario projects a 60:40 ratio by 2025, favoring in situ processes.[28] Both processes are briefly discussed below.

Mining

Oil sands deposits that are less than about 250 feet below the surface can be removed using conventional strip-mining methods. The strip-mining process includes removal of the overburden

---

[27] Canadian Association of Petroleum Producers (CAPP), *Crude Oil Forecast, Markets & Pipelines*, June 2011.

[28] Canadian Association of Petroleum Producers (CAPP), *Crude Oil Forecast, Markets & Pipelines*, June 2011.

(i.e., primary soils and vegetation), excavation of the resource, and transportation to a processing facility.

In Situ

Oil sands deposits that are deeper than 75 meters are recovered using one of three in situ methods: primary production,[29] cyclic steam stimulation (CSS), and steam-assisted gravity drainage (SAGD). CSS and SAGD, which accounted for approximately 75% of Alberta's in situ recovery in 2010, involve injecting steam into an oil sands reservoir.[30] The steam heats the bitumen, decreasing its viscosity and enabling its collection. Based on 2010 data, SAGD accounts for the greatest percentage of in situ recovery and is the preferred method of recovery for most new projects.[31] SADG involves a top well for steam injection and a bottom well for bitumen production.[32] **Figure 5** provides an illustration of this process.

Figure 5. Illustration of Steam-Assisted Gravity Drainage (SAGD)

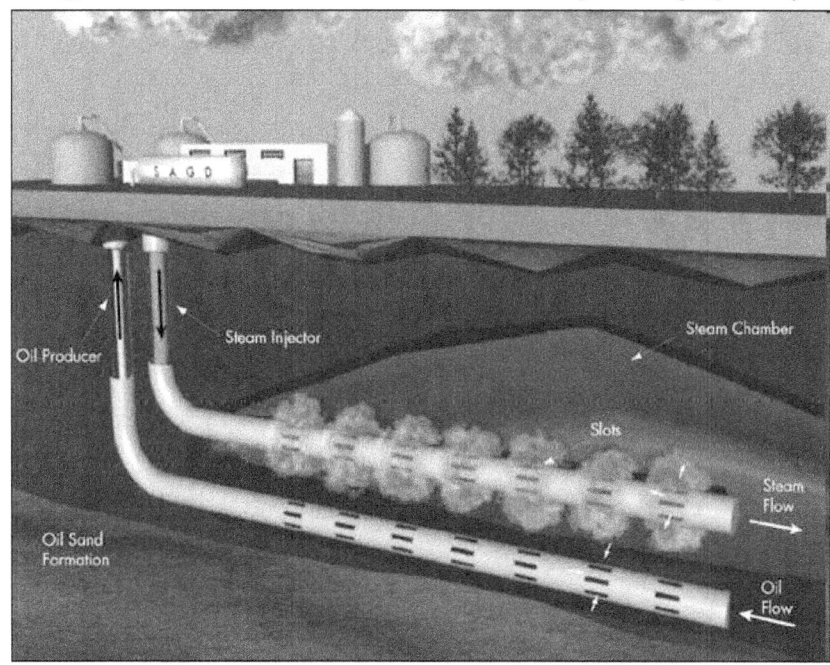

Source: Pembina Institute, at http://www.pembina.org.

---

[29] According to the Energy Resource Conservation Board (ERCB), "Primary production includes those schemes that use water and polymer injection as a recovery method." *Alberta's Energy Reserves 2010 and Supply/Demand Outlook 2011-2020*, 2011.

[30] ERCB, 2011.

[31] ERCB, 2011

[32] In contrast, CSS uses a vertical well to liquefy the bitumen, which is then pumped to the surface using the same well.

Properties of Oil Sands-Derived Crudes Compared to Other Crudes

Crude oil is a complex mix of hydrocarbons, ranging from simple compounds with small molecules and low densities to very dense compounds with extremely large molecules. Three key properties of crude oils include the following:

- **API Gravity.** API[33] Gravity measures the weight of a crude oil compared to water. It is reported in degrees (°) by convention. API gravities above 10° indicate crude oils lighter than water (they float); API gravities below 10° indicate crude oils heavier than water (they sink). Although the definition of "heavy" crude oil may vary, it is generally defined by refiners as being at or below 22.3° API gravity.[34]

- **Sulfur Content.** Sulfur content in crude oil is an indication of potential corrosiveness due to the presence of acidic sulfur compounds. Sulfur content is measured as an overall percentage of free sulfur and sulfur compounds in a crude oil by weight. Total sulfur content in crude oils generally ranges from below 0.05% to 5.0%. Crudes with more than 1.0% free sulfur or other sulfur-containing compounds are typically referred to as "sour," below 0.5% sulfur as "sweet."[35]

- **Total Acid Number.** Total Acid Number (TAN) measures the composition of acids in a crude which can gauge its potential for corrosion, particularly in a refinery. TAN value is measured as the number of milligrams (mg) of potassium hydroxide (KOH) needed to neutralize the acids in one gram of oil. As a rule-of-thumb, crude oils with a TAN greater than 0.5 are considered to be potentially corrosive due to the presence of naphthenic acids.[36]

Table 1 compares Alberta's different oil sands crudes with other crude oils extracted in the United States and around the world. The data indicate that all oil sands crudes would be considered heavy crudes. Heavy crudes are found throughout the world, including the United States. The data indicate that oil sands crudes resemble other heavy crudes in terms of sulfur content and TAN.

---

[33] American Petroleum Institute.

[34] U.S. Energy Information Administration, Crude Oil Input Qualities, "Definitions, Sources and Explanatory Notes," web page, July 28, 2011, http://www.eia.gov/dnav/pet/TblDefs/pet_pnp_crq_tbldef2.asp. In the marine tanker industry, heavy grade crudes are defined as crudes with an API below 25.7 , as bitumen emulsions, or as certain viscous fuel oils. See McQuilling Services, LLC, "Carriage of Heavy Grade Oil," Garden City, NY, 2011, http://www.meglobaloil.com/MARPOL.pdf.

[35] JDL Oil and Gas Exploration, Inc., "Crude Oil Basics," web page, July 28, 2011, http://www.jdloil.com/oil_basics.htm.

[36] R.D. Kane and M.S. Cayard, "A Comprehensive Study of Naphthenic Acid Corrosion," Paper No. 02555, Corrosion 2002, http://www.icorr.net/wp-content/uploads/2011/01/napthenic_corrosion.pdf.

Table 1. Selected Global Crude Oil Specifications

Source	Crude Oil Name	°API Gravity	Sulfur (Weight %)	TAN (mgKOH/g)
Alberta Oil Sands Crude Oils				
- Dilbits	Access Western Blend	21.9	3.94	1.70
	Cold Lake	20.9	3.78	0.97
	Peace River Heavy	20.8	4.97	2.49
	Seal Heavy	20.5	4.64	1.86
	Smiley Coleville	20.0	2.98	0.97
	Wabasca Heavy	20.3	4.10	1.03
	Western Canadian Select	20.6	3.46	0.92
- DilSynBit	A bian Heavy	19.1	2.42	0.51
Selected Heavy Crude Oils				
Western Canada	Western Canadian Blend	20.7	3.16	0.71
U.S. (California)	Hondo Monterey	19.4	4.70	0.43
	Kern River	13.4	1.10	2.36
Venezuela	Pilon	16.2	2.47	1.60
	Bachaquero	13.5	2.30	2.63
	Tia Juana Heavy	12.3	2.82	3.90
	Laguna	10.9	2.66	2.82
	Boscan	10.1	5.40	0.91
Mexico	Maya	21.5	3.31	0.43
Italy	Tempa Rossa	20.4	5.44	0.05
United Kingdom	Captain	19.2	0.70	2.40
Indonesia	Duri (Sumatran Heavy)	20.8	0.20	1.27
Selected Medium and Light Crude Oils (> 22.3° API)				
U.S. (Alaska)	Alaskan North Slope	32.1	0.93	0.12
U.S. (Texas)	West Texas Intermediate	40.8	0.34	0.10
U.S. (Gu f of Mexico)	Hoops Blend	31.6	1.15	1.07
	Thunderhorse	28.3	0.64	0.47
	Poseidon Heavy-sour	29.7	1.65	0.41
	Mars Heavy-sour	28.9	2.05	0.51
	Southern Green Canyon Heavy-Sour	28.4	2.48	0.17
Nigeria	Bonga	30.2	0.25	0.55
Norway	Statfjord	28.3	0.64	0.47
Dubai	Dubai Fateh Heavy	30.8	2.07	0.05
Saudi Arabia	Arabian Heavy	27.5	2.95	0.40
	Arabian Light	33.7	1.96	0.05

Sources: Canadian crude data from Crude Quality Inc., Canadian Crude Quick Reference Guide, Updated June 2, 2011, at http://www.crudemonitor.ca; Other crude oil data from: Capline, Crude Oil Assays, at http://www.cap inepipe ine.com; BP Crude Assays, at http://www.bp.com; ExxonMobil, at http://www.exxonmobil.com/crudeoil/about_crudes_region.aspx; "Benchmark West Texas Intermediate Crude Assayed," *Oil and Gas Journal*, 1994; McQuilling Services, LLC, "Carriage of Heavy Grade Oil," Garden City, NY, 2011, http://www.meglobaloil.com/MARPOL.pdf; Hydrocarbon Pub ishing Co., *Opportunity Crudes Report II*, Southeastern, PA, 2011, p. 5, http://www.hydrocarbonpublishing.com/ReportP/Prospectus-Opportunity%20Crudes%20II_2011.pdf.

Notes: The crude oils listed above are not an exhaustive list, nor do they represent a specific percentage of global consumption. The crudes listed above are selected examples of different crude oils from around the world. Multiple crude oils from Venezuela are included to indicate the range of parameters in different heavy crude oils.

Section 2: Keystone XL Pipeline—Overview

As originally proposed by TransCanada in September 2008,[37] the Keystone XL pipeline would involve two major segments (**Figure 6**). The first segment—approximately 850 pipeline miles in the United States[38]—would cross the U.S.-Canadian border into Montana, pass through South Dakota, and terminate in Steele City, Nebraska. The second segment—approximately 480 miles and labeled as the "Gulf Coast Project" in **Figure 6**—would connect an existing pipeline in Cushing, Oklahoma with locations in southern Texas.[39]

As discussed below, the Department of State (DOS) announced its denial of the Keystone XL permit in January 2012. In February 2012, TransCanada announced that it would proceed with development of the southern pipeline segment as a separate proposal. As this segment is within the United States, it does not require a Presidential Permit (discussed below). Thus, the revised permit, which TransCanada submitted on May 12, 2012, only applies to the first segment that connects Canada with the United States.

The Keystone XL pipeline would have the capacity to deliver 830,000 barrels per day (bpd), a substantial flow rate compared to other U.S.-Canada import pipelines (**Table 3**).The 36-inch-diameter pipeline would require a 50-foot-wide permanent right-of-way along the route. Approximately 95% of the pipeline right-of-way would be on privately owned land, with the remaining 5% almost equally state and federal land. Private land uses are primarily agricultural—farmers and cattle ranchers. Above ground facilities associated with the pipelines include pump stations (with associated electric transmission interconnection facilities), mainline valves, and delivery metering facilities.

The Keystone XL pipeline and the "Gulf Coast Project" would combine with two existing pipeline segments to complete TransCanada's Keystone Pipeline System. This system is depicted in **Figure 6**. These existing segments include:

- The Keystone Mainline: A 30-inch pipeline with a capacity of nearly 600,000 bpd that connects Alberta oil sands to U.S. refineries in Illinois. The U.S. portion runs 1,086 miles and begins at the international border in North Dakota. The Keystone Mainline began operating in June 2010.

- The Keystone Cushing Extension: A 36-inch pipeline that runs 298 miles from Steele City, Nebraska to existing crude oil terminals and tanks farms in Cushing, Oklahoma. The Cushing Extension began operating February 2011.

---

[37] The original application and related documents are available at the Department of State Keystone XL website, at http://keystonepipeline-xl.state.gov/archive/index.htm.

[38] 1,183 miles from its origin in Alberta, Canada. See U.S. Department of State, *Final Environmental Impact Statement for the Proposed Keystone XL Project*, August 2011.

[39] An additional 50-mile segment would connect to additional locations in Texas. For further details, see U.S. Department of State, *Final Environmental Impact Statement for the Proposed Keystone XL Project*, August 2011.

Figure 6. The Keystone Pipeline System

Completed and Proposed Segments of the Keystone and Keystone XL Pipelines

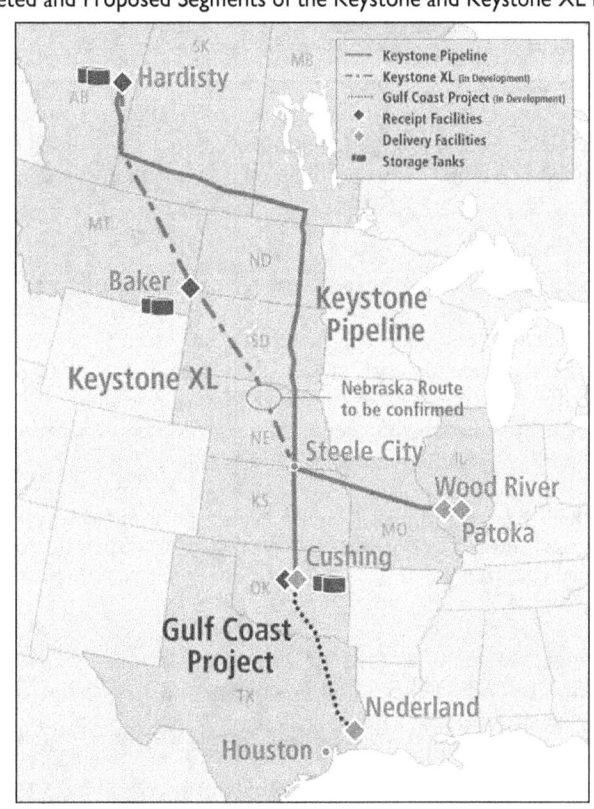

Source: TransCanada.

Federal Requirements to Consider the Pipeline's Environmental Impacts

When considering a Presidential Permit application, the DOS must conduct an environmental review of its actions pursuant to the National Environmental Policy Act (NEPA, 42 U.S.C. §4321 et seq.). This process highlighted many environmental impacts associated with the construction, operation, and maintenance of the pipeline system and associated facilities.

Issues that arose and environmental impacts identified during DOS efforts to process TransCanada's application for a Presidential Permit ultimately resulted in the denial of its permit application. With TransCanada's May 4, 2012 reapplication for a permit to construct the Keystone XL pipeline project, the Presidential Permit process and NEPA compliance process begin anew.

Generally, federal agencies have no authority to control siting of oil pipelines, even interstate pipelines.[40] Instead, the primary siting authority for oil pipelines generally would be established

---

[40] This is in contrast to interstate natural gas pipelines, which, under Section 7(c) (15 USC §717f(c)) of the Natural Gas Act, must obtain a "certificate of public convenience and necessity" from the Federal Energy Regulatory Commission.

under applicable state law (which may vary considerably from state to state).[41] However, in accordance with Executive Order 13337, a facility connecting the United States with a foreign country, including a pipeline, requires a Presidential Permit from DOS before it can proceed.[42]

Key elements of the Presidential Permit process, including DOS efforts to identify environmental impacts associated with the TransCanada's 2008 permit application are discussed below. Included in that discussion are relevant activities and requirements associated with DOS compliance with NEPA and its obligation to determine whether the proposed pipeline would serve the national interest.

Presidential Permit Requirements for Cross-Border Pipelines

A decision to issue or deny a Presidential Permit application is based on a determination that the proposed project would serve the "national interest." This term is not defined in the Executive Orders. In the course of making that determination, DOS may consider a wide range of factors such as the project's potential impacts to the environment, economy, energy security, foreign policy, and others. Regarding its determination, DOS has stated:

> Consistent with the President's broad discretion in the conduct of foreign affairs, DOS has significant discretion in the factors it examines in making a National Interest Determination. The factors examined and the approaches to their examination are not necessarily the same from project to project.[43]

However, the Department has identified the following as key factors it considered in making *previous* national interest determinations for oil pipeline permit applications:

- Environmental impacts of the proposed projects;

- Impacts of the proposed projects on the diversity of supply to meet U.S. crude oil demand and energy needs;

- The security of transport pathways for crude oil supplies to the United States through import facilities constructed at the border relative to other modes of transport;

- Stability of trading partners from whom the United States obtains crude oil;

---

[41] Federal laws and regulations address other matters, including worker safety and environmental concerns. See CRS Report R41536, *Keeping America's Pipelines Safe and Secure Key Issues for Congress*, by Paul W. Parfomak and CRS Report RL33705, *Oil Spills in U.S. Coastal Waters Background and Governance*, by Jonathan L. Ramseur.

[42] This authority was originally vested in the U.S. State Department with the promulgation of Executive Order 11423, "Providing for the performance of certain functions heretofore performed by the President with respect to certain facilities constructed and maintained on the borders of the United States," in 1968. Executive Order 13337, "Issuance of Permits With Respect to Certain Energy-Related Facilities and Land Transportation Crossings on the International Boundaries of the United States," of April 30, 2004, amended this authority and the procedures associated with permit review for energy-related projects, but did not substantially alter the exercise of authority or the delegation to the Secretary of State in E.O. 11423. Due to the particular significance to Presidential Permit issuance for pipelines, provisions in E.O 13337 will be cited in this report. For further information on the Executive Order authority and related issues, see CRS Report R42124, *Proposed Keystone XL Pipeline Legal Issues*, by Adam Vann et al.

[43] The U.S. State Department, *Final Environmental Impact Statement for the Keystone XL Project*, August 2011, "Introduction" (as amended September 22, 2011), p. 1-4, available at http://keystonepipeline-xl.state.gov/archive/dos_docs/feis/index.htm#.

- Relationship between the United States and various foreign suppliers of crude oil and the ability of the United States to work with those countries to meet overall environmental and energy security goals;

- Impact of proposed projects on broader foreign policy objectives, including a comprehensive strategy to address climate change;

- Economic benefits to the United States of constructing and operating proposed projects; and

- relationships between proposed projects and goals to reduce reliance on fossil fuels and to increase use of alternative and renewable energy sources.[44]

DOS may consider additional factors to inform its national interest determination for a given project. However, pursuant to E.O. 13337, for each permit application it receives for an energy-related project, DOS must request the views of the Attorney General, Administrator of the Environmental Protection Agency (EPA), and Secretaries of Defense, the Interior, Commerce, Transportation, Energy, and Homeland Security (or the heads of those departments or agencies with relevant authority or responsibility over relevant elements of the proposed project). DOS may request the views of additional federal department and agency heads, as well as additional local, state, or tribal agencies, as it deems appropriate for a given project. DOS must also invite public comment on the proposed project.

If, after considering the views and assistance of various agencies and the comments from the public, DOS finds that issuance of a permit would serve the national interest, then a Presidential Permit may be issued. Specific to the Keystone XL pipeline, in its May 2012 Presidential Permit application, TransCanada states

> The project will serve the national interest of the United States by providing a secure and reliable source of Canadian crude oil to meet the demand from refineries and markets in the United States, by providing critically important market access to developing domestic oil supplies in the Bakken formation in Montana and North Dakota, and by reducing U.S. reliance on crude oil supplies from Venezuela, Mexico, the Middle East, and Africa. The project will also provide significant economic and employment benefits to the United States, with minimal impacts on the environment.[45]

It is during the NEPA process that DOS will determine the degree to which the proposed pipeline project may impact the environment, as well as identify potential mitigation measures or protections necessary to reduce the potential for adverse environmental impacts. When the NEPA process is complete, DOS may use that assessment of environmental impacts, with other factors, to determine if the project does, in fact, serve the national interest.

---

[44] Ibid.

[45] TransCanada Keystone Pipeline, L.P., "Application of TransCanada Keystone Pipeline L.P. for a Presidential Permit Authorizing the Construction, Operation, and Maintenance of Pipeline Facilities for the Importation of Crude Oil to be Located at the United States-Canada Border," U.S. Dept. of State, May 4, 2012, pp. 1-2, available at http://www.keystonepipeline-xl.state.gov/.

Identification of Environmental Impacts During the NEPA Process [46]

The DOS review of a Presidential Permit application explicitly requires compliance with multiple federal environmental statutes.[47] Environmental requirements identified within the context of the NEPA process has drawn considerable attention.

Pursuant to NEPA, in considering an application for a Presidential Permit, DOS must take into account environmental impacts of a proposed facility and directly related construction. In complying with NEPA, federal agencies must prepare an Environmental Impact Statement (EIS) for projects determined to have "significant" environmental impacts. DOS concluded that issuance of a Presidential Permit for the proposed construction, connection, operation, and maintenance of the Keystone XL Pipeline and its associated facilities at the United States border may have a significant impact on the environment within the meaning of NEPA.[48] As a result, DOS prepared an EIS to identify the reasonably foreseeable impacts from the proposed Keystone XL pipeline.[49] Similarly, an EIS will likely be required for the pipeline project for which the May 4, 2012 permit application was filed.

EIS preparation is done in two stages, resulting in a draft and final EIS. NEPA regulations require the draft EIS to be circulated for public and agency comment, followed by a final EIS that incorporates those comments.[50] The agency responsible for preparing the EIS, in this case DOS, is designated the "lead agency." In developing the EIS, DOS must rely on information provided by TransCanada. For example, TransCanada's original permit application included an Environmental Report which was intended to provide the State Department with sufficient information to understand the scope of potential environmental impacts of the project.[51]

In preparing the draft EIS, the lead agency must request input from "cooperating agencies," which include any agency with jurisdiction by law or with special expertise regarding any environmental impact associated with the project.[52] The original Keystone XL permit process involved 11 federal cooperating agencies, including the Environmental Protection Agency (EPA),

---

[46] For more detailed NEPA information, see CRS Report RL33152, *The National Environmental Policy Act (NEPA) Background and Implementation*, by Linda Luther.

[47] DOS is explicitly directed to review the project's compliance with the National Historic Preservation Act (16 U.S.C. §470f), the Endangered Species Act (16 U.S.C. §1531 et seq.), and Executive Order 12898 of February 11, 1994 (59 *Federal Register* 7629), concerning environmental justice.

[48] U.S. Department of State, "Notice of Intent to Prepare an Environmental Impact Statement and to Conduct Scoping Meetings and Notice of Floodplain and Wetland Involvement and to Initiate Consultation under Section 106 of the National Historic Preservation Act for the Proposed TransCanada Keystone XL Pipeline," 74 *Federal Register* 5020, January 28, 2009.

[49] In preparing an EIS associated with a Presidential Permit application, NEPA regulations promulgated by both the Council of Environmental Quality (CEQ) and the State Department would apply to the proposed project. CEQ regulations implementing NEPA (under 40 C.F.R. §§1500-1508) apply to all federal agencies. NEPA regulations applicable to State Department actions, which supplement the CEQ regulations, are found at 22 C.F.R. §161.

[50] For information regarding NEPA requirements, see CRS Report RL33152, *The National Environmental Policy Act (NEPA) Background and Implementation*, by Linda Luther.

[51] Documents submitted by TransCanada for its initial 2008 Presidential Permit application, now archived by DOS, are available at http://keystonepipeline-xl.state.gov/archive/proj_docs/index.htm.

[52] 40 C.F.R. §1508.5. Also, Executive Order 13337 directs the Secretary of State to refer an application for a Presidential Permit to other specifically identified federal departments and agencies on whether granting the application would be in the national interest.

---

as well as state agencies. **Table A-1** (in the **Appendix**) provides a list of various agencies and their roles in the pipeline permitting process.

In addition to its role as a cooperating agency, EPA is also required to review and comment publicly on the EIS and rate both the adequacy of the EIS itself and the level of environmental impact of the proposed project.[53] EPA's role in rating draft EISs for the Keystone XL pipeline project had a significant impact on the NEPA process for TransCanada's 2008 Presidential Permit application.

The State Department released its draft EIS for the proposed Keystone XL Pipeline project for public comment on April 16, 2010.[54] On July 16, 2010, EPA rated the draft EIS "Inadequate."[55] EPA found that potentially significant impacts were not evaluated and that the additional information and analysis needed was of such importance that the draft EIS would need to be formally revised and again made available for public review. DOS issued a supplemental draft EIS on April 15, 2011.[56] In addition to addressing issues associated with EPA's inadequacy rating, the supplemental draft EIS addressed comments received from other agencies and the public. On June 6, 2011, EPA sent a letter to the State Department that rated the supplemental draft EIS as having "Insufficient Information" and having "Environmental Objections" to the proposed action.[57] EPA acknowledged that DOS had "worked diligently" to develop additional information in response to EPA's comments on the draft EIS, but additional analysis was needed on several points, including potential oil spill risks and lifecycle greenhouse gas emissions associated with the proposed project.

In its June 6, 2011 letter, EPA refers to agreements with DOS that certain deficiencies identified in the supplemental draft EIS would be addressed in the final EIS. On August 26, 2011, DOS did issue the final EIS for the proposed Keystone XL Pipeline (hereafter referred to as 2011 FEIS).[58] Although DOS addressed stakeholder comments, including those of EPA, in its 2011 FEIS,[59] it is unknown whether EPA made any additional comments to DOS during the 90-day public review period marking the national interest determination (discussed below). Regardless, EPA will have

---

[53] Rating the EIS takes place after the draft is issued. The EIS could be rated either "Adequate," "Insufficient Information," or "Inadequate." EPA's rating of a project's environmental impacts may range from "Lack of Objections" to "Environmentally Unsatisfactory." In rating the impact of the action itself, EPA would specify one of the following: "Lack of Objections," "Environmental Concerns," "Environmental Objections," or "Environmentally Unsatisfactory." The federal agency would then be required to respond to EPA's rating, as appropriate. For more information, see the U.S. Environmental Protection Agency's "Environmental Impact Statement (EIS) Rating System Criteria" at http://www.epa.gov/compliance/nepa/comments/ratings.html.

[54] EISs prepared by DOS for TransCanada's 2008 Presidential Permit application, now archived by DOS, are available at http://keystonepipeline-xl.state.gov/archive/dos_docs/index.htm.

[55] U.S. Environmental Protection Agency's July 16, 2010, letter to the U.S. Department of State commenting on the draft EIS for the Keystone XL project is available at http://yosemite.epa.gov/oeca/webeis.nsf/%28PDFView%29/20100126/$file/20100126.PDF.

[56] See footnote 54.

[57] U.S. Environmental Protection Agency's June 6, 2011 letter to the U.S. Department of State commenting on the supplemental draft EIS for the Keystone XL project is available at http://yosemite.epa.gov/oeca/webeis.nsf/%28PDFView%29/20110125/$file/20110125.PDF?OpenElement.

[58] U.S. Department of State, *Final Environmental Impact Statement for the Proposed Keystone XL Project*, August 26, 2011 (with portions amended September 22, 2011), available at http://keystonepipeline-xl.state.gov/archive/dos_docs/feis/index.htm.

[59] 2011 final EIS, "Appendix A, Responses to Comments and Scoping Summary Report," available at http://keystonepipeline-xl.state.gov/archive/dos_docs/feis/vol3and4/appendixa/index.htm.

---

an opportunity to comment on NEPA documentation prepared for TransCanada's May 2012 permit application.

Identification of Environmental Impacts During the National Interest Determination

Generally, the NEPA review is considered complete when (or if) the federal agency issues a final Record of Decision (ROD), formalizing the selection of a project alternative. However, for a project subject to a Presidential Permit, issuance of a final EIS marks the beginning of a 90-day public review period during which DOS gathers additional information necessary to make its national interest determination. For previous Presidential Permits, a ROD and National Interest Determination were issued as the same document.[60]

Issuance of the ROD and National Interest Determination involve distinctly different, yet interrelated requirements. Under NEPA, DOS must fully assess the environmental consequences of an action and potential project alternatives *before* making a final decision. NEPA does not prohibit a federal action that has adverse environment impacts; it requires only that a federal agency be fully *aware of* and *consider* those adverse impacts before selecting a final project alternative. That is, NEPA is intended to be part of the decision-making process, not dictate a particular outcome.

The DOS's national interest determination, however, does dictate a particular outcome—approval or denial of a Presidential Permit. Issuance of a Presidential Permit is predicated on the finding that the proposed project would serve the national interest. While NEPA does not prohibit federal actions with adverse environmental impacts, a project's adverse environmental impacts may lead the DOS to determine that the project is not in the national interest.

Table 2 summarizes milestones in the national interest determination for TransCanada's initial permit application.[61]

---

[60] U.S. Department of State, *Department of State Record of Decision and National Interest Determination, TransCanada Keystone Pipeline, LP Application for Presidential Permit*, February 25, 2008.

[61] A more comprehensive timeline is provided in CRS Report R41668, *Keystone XL Pipeline Project Key Issues*, by Paul W. Parfomak, Linda Luther, and Adam Vann.

Table 2. Milestones in the Keystone XL Pipeline National Interest Determination
Administrative, Congressional, State, and Company Actions

Date	Description
2011	
August 26	DOS issues its FEIS; the 90-day public review period for the National Interest Determination begins.
October 24	The Governor of Nebraska calls the state legislature into a special session to determine if siting legislation can be crafted and passed for pipeline routing in Nebraska.
November 10	DOS announces that additional information will be needed regarding alternative pipeline routes that would avoid the Nebraska Sand Hills before National Interest Determination can be made. Officials suggest that analysis needed to prepare the supplemental EIS, including additional public comment, could be completed as early as the first quarter of 2013.
November 14	TransCanada announces that it will work with the Nebraska Department of Environmental Quality (DEQ) to identify a potential pipeine route that would avoid the Nebraska Sand Hills.
November 22	The Governor of Nebraska signs legislation passed during the special session directing the Nebraska DEQ to work collaboratively with the State Department to gather information necessary for a supplemental EIS.
December 23	The Temporary Payroll Tax Cut Continuation Act of 2011 (P.L. 112-78) is enacted, including provisions requiring the Secretary of State to issue a permit for the project within 60 days, unless the President determines the project is not in the national interest.
2012	
January 18	DOS announces, with the President's consent, that it will deny the Keystone XL permit. It states that its decision was predicated on the fact that the 60-day deadline under P.L. 112-78 did not provide sufficient time to obtain information necessary to assess the current project's national interest.
February 3	DOS issues the formal permit denial in the *Federal Register* (Vol. 77, p. 5614), which included a Memorandum from the President stating that the project would, "at this time ... not serve the national interest."
February 27	TransCanada announced that it would proceed with development of the southern pipeline segment as a separate proposal. This segment would connect Cushing, Oklahoma with points in southern Texas. As it would not cross the U.S. border, it would not require a Presidential Permit.
April 19	TransCanada submits to the Nebraska DEQ an initial analysis of alternative Keystone XL pipeline routes that avoid the Sand Hills. **Figure A-1** illustrates these options, which are still under consideration.
May 4	A new Presidential Permit application is submitted to DOS reflecting new information regarding alternative pipeline routes through Nebraska. The NEPA process for the new project begins, potentially drawing upon relevant documents from the 2011 final EIS.

Source: The Congressional Research Service, based on a review of events during, and affecting, the NEPA process conducted for the 2008 Presidential Permit application for the Keystone XL pipeline project, including TransCanada Corp., Media Advisory, "State of Nebraska to Play Major Role in Defining New Keystone XL Route Away From the Sandhills," November 14, 2011; U.S. Department of State, press release, "Denial of the Keystone XL Pipeline Appication," January 18, 2012 and "Keystone XL Final Environmental Impact Statement Released; Public Meetings Set," available at http://www.state.gov/r/pa/prs/ps/2012/01/181473.htm.

Consideration of Environmental Impacts Outside of the United States

With regard to compliance requirements under NEPA, DOS is not required to identify or analyze environmental impacts that occur within another sovereign nation that result from actions approved by that sovereign nation. However, to further the purpose of the NEPA, Executive Order 12114 "Environmental Effects Abroad of Major Federal Actions," requires federal agencies to prepare an analysis of significant impacts from a federal action abroad. This order does not, however, require federal agencies to evaluate the impacts of projects outside the United States when that project is undertaken with the involvement or participation of the foreign nation in which the project is undertaken—as is the case with Canada's participation in the Keystone XL pipeline project. While it is not subject to it, as a matter of policy, DOS uses the order as guidance and includes information in the final EIS regarding the environmental analysis conducted by the Canadian government.

Apart from any obligation under NEPA, however, DOS may take into consideration extraterritorial project impacts, as it deems necessary, as part of its national interest determination. For example, as noted above, factors DOS considered in making its determination for past pipeline projects included the proposed project's impact on broader policy objectives, including a comprehensive strategy to address climate change, and the relationships between the proposed project and U.S. goals to reduce reliance on fossil fuels and to increase use of alternative and renewable energy sources. In its January 2012 denial of TransCanada's initial Presidential Permit application, DOS did not specifically cite these issues as playing a role in its determination. However, it is likely that they will continue to be factors of concern to project opponents.

As discussed below, opponents of the pipeline proposal have expressed concern over environmental impacts outside of the United States that may occur as a direct or indirect result of the pipeline's construction. When it denied TransCanada's initial permit application, DOS did not cite environmental impacts outside the United States among the factors contributing to that decision. The degree to which environmental impacts abroad may have influenced that initial permit denial is unclear. In processing TransCanada's 2012 permit application, it may be assumed that DOS will consider environmental impacts abroad as it did for the 2008 permit application.

Other Oil Pipelines from Canada

As illustrated in **Figure 7**, multiple pipelines connect Canadian oil resources with the United States. Several of these pipelines have been constructed in recent years.

Figure 7. Oil Pipelines between Canada and the United States

Existing and Proposed

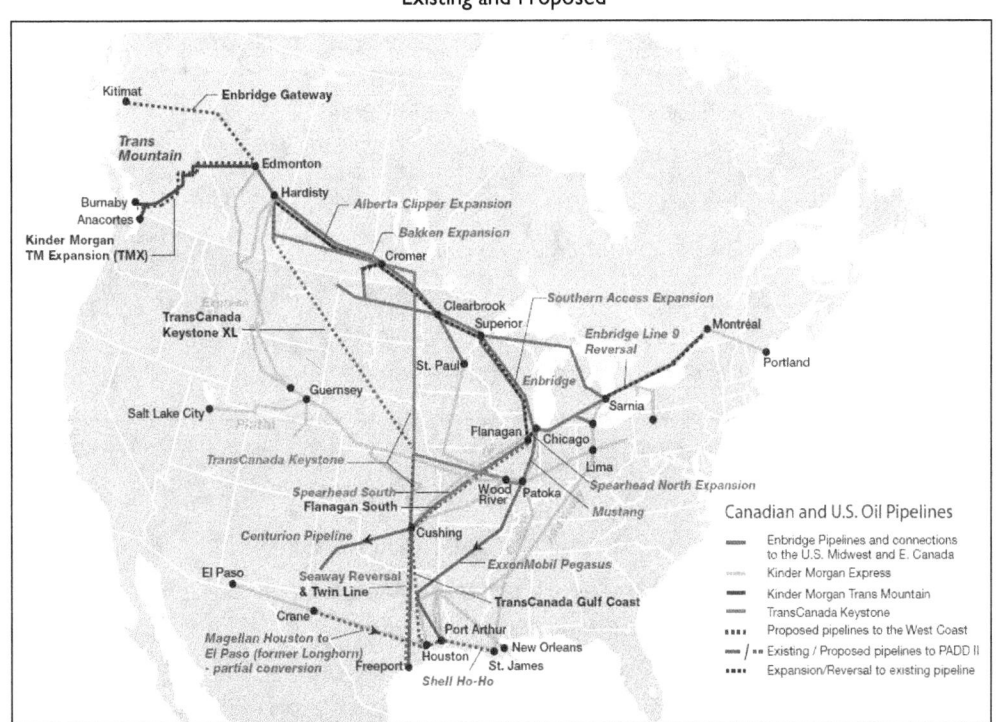

Source: Canadian Association of Petroleum Producers, *Crude Oil: Forecast, Markets & Pipelines*, June 2012.

Notes: The Keystone XL route in this figure identifies the developer's originally proposed "preferred alternative." As noted above, the route through Nebraska is expected to change.

Table 3 identifies pipelines that have applied for a Presidential Permit in the past six years. The table indicates that the Keystone XL permit process timetable, which is ongoing, has substantially exceeded prior permit process timetables.

Table 3. Major U.S.-Canadian Petroleum Import Pipelines

Presidential Permit Activity (2006 – Present)

Pipeline	Operator	Permit Submitted	EIS Prepared?	Permit Issued	First Year of Operation	Capacity (bpd)
Southern Lights (LSr)[a]	Southern Lights	April 2007	No	June 2008	2009	186,000
Keystone[b]	TransCanada	April 2006	Yes	March 2008	2010	591,000
Alberta C ipper[c]	Enbridge	May 2007	Yes	August 2009	2010	450,000
Keystone XL[d]	TransCanada	September 2008	Yes	Denied January 2012	NA	830,000
Keystone XL[d]	TransCanada	May 2012	Forthcoming[e]			

Source: Prepared by CRS; pipe ine status and capacity information from CAPP, 201 1. More specific sources identified below.

Notes:

a. 72 *Federal Register* 41383, July 27, 2007; 73 *Federal Register* 32620, June 9, 2008.

b. Department of State website, at http://www.keystonepipe ine.state.gov.

c. Department of State website, at http://www.albertac ipper.state.gov.

d. Department of State website, at http://www.keystonepipe ine-xl.state.gov.

e. Although no new decision deadline was estab ished, in November 201 1, State Department officials suggested that it would be "reasonable to expect that this process including a public comment period on a supplement to the final EIS consistent with NEPA could be completed as early as the first quarter of 2013." See http://www.state.gov/r/pa/prs/ps/201 1/1 1/176964.htm.

When DOS issued the Presidential Permit for the first Keystone pipeline project in 2008, DOS concluded that the project "would result in limited adverse environmental impacts" and would serve the national interests of the United States for the following reasons:

> It increases the diversity of available supplies among the United States' worldwide crude oil sources. Increased output from the [Western Canada Sedimentary Basin] can be utilized by a growing number of refineries in the United States that have access and means of transport for these increased supplies.

> It shortens the transportation pathway for a portion of United States crude oil imports. Crude oil supplies in Western Canada represent the largest and closest foreign supply source to domestic refineries that do not require marine transportation.

> It increases crude oil supplies from a source region that has been a stable and reliable trading partner of the United States and does not require exposure of crude oil in high seas transport and railway routes that may be affected by heightened security and environmental concerns.

> It provides additional supplies of crude oil to make up for the continued decline in imports from several other major U.S. suppliers.[62]

---

[62] DOS, *Record of Decision and National Interest Determination, Keystone Pipeline*, 2008, at
(continued...)

Proponents of the Keystone XL pipeline may point to these statements as reasons to issue a Presidential Permit to the XL proposal.

Section 3: Selected Environmental Issues

The environmental issues raised by opponents of the Keystone XL pipeline cover a wide range. These issues involve both local/regional concerns—some in the United States, some in Canada—and national/global concerns. The variety of issues raised by pipeline opponents suggest that the stakeholders are not a monolithic group.

This section does not provide an exhaustive list of environmental issues raised by opponents of the pipeline proposal. Instead, this section discusses several issues that (1) appear to be central to stakeholder opposition and (2) relate to the material that would be transported in the pipeline: oil sands crude oil. These selected environmental issues include the following:

- Greenhouse gas emissions intensity;

- Climate change policy;

- Oil spill risk; and

- Oil sands extraction impacts

GHG Emissions Intensity of Oil Sands Crude Oils[63]

Greenhouse gas (GHG) emissions, primarily carbon dioxide (CO_2) and methane, are emitted during a variety of stages in oil sands production. Although all fossil fuel development activities—and other forms of energy to varying degrees—emit GHG emissions, opponents of the Keystone XL pipeline contend that oil sands have a higher emissions intensity than other forms of crude oil.[64] In this context, emissions intensity means GHG emissions per units of production (e.g., barrels or energy).

Industry stakeholders argue that this conclusion is overstated, asserting that GHG emissions from oil sands crude oil are comparable to some other global crudes, some of which are produced and/or consumed in the United States.[65] The issue has generated considerable debate, attention, and analyses from multiple parties.

This section (1) describes the tool—life-cycle assessments—used for comparisons; (2) discusses the oil sands life-cycle assessment results; and (3) compares oil sands emissions intensities with other crude oils.

(...continued)

http://www.cardnoentrix.com/keystone/project/SignedROD.pdf.

[63] This section is an abridged version of CRS Report R42537, *Canadian Oil Sands Life-Cycle Assessments of Greenhouse Gas Emissions*, by Richard K. Lattanzio.

[64] See e.g., NRDC, *Setting the Record Straight Lifecycle Emissions of Tar Sands*, November 2010.

[65] See e.g., Canadian Association of Petroleum Producers, *The Facts on Oil Sands*, April 2012, at http://www.capp.ca.

Life-Cycle Assessments

A life-cycle assessment (LCA) is an analytic method used for evaluating and comparing the environmental impacts of various products.[66] LCAs can be used to identify, quantify, and track emissions of CO_2 and other GHG emissions arising from the development of hydrocarbon resources, and to express them in a single, universal metric: carbon dioxide equivalent (CO_2e) per unit of fuel or fuel use.[67] The results of an LCA can be used to evaluate the GHG emissions intensity of various stages of the fuel's life cycle, as well as to compare the emissions intensity of one type of fuel or method of production to another.

GHG emissions profiles modeled by most LCAs are based on a set of boundaries commonly referred to as "cradle-to-grave," or, in the case of transportation fuels such as petroleum, "Well-to-Wheel" (WTW). WTW assessments for petroleum-based transportation fuels focus on the emissions associated with the entire life cycle of the fuel. This includes:

- extraction;
- transportation;
- upgrading and/or refining;
- distribution of refined product (e.g., gasoline, diesel, jet fuel); and
- combustion of the fuel.

Inclusion of the final combustion phase allows for the most complete picture of crude oil's impact on GHG emissions, as this phase can contribute up to 70%-80% of WTW emissions. However, other LCAs, such as well-to-tank (WTT) assessments, may focus solely on production and/or extraction.

Both study types are valid, but they tell different stories. Oil sands opponents often highlight results from WTT studies, because results from WTT comparisons show oil sands crudes' emissions intensities to be considerably higher than conventional oils. Oil sands proponents often point to WTT results: the emission intensity differences are less pronounced due to the inclusion of the combustion phase.

GHG Life-Cycle Assessments of Canadian Oil Sands

A number of published and publicly available studies have attempted to assess the life-cycle GHG emissions data for Canadian oil sands crudes. The studies examined in this report include the LCAs analyzed by DOS in its 2011 FEIS. A CRS survey of these studies reveals the following:

1. Canadian oil sands crudes are, on average, somewhat more GHG emission-intensive than the crudes they would displace in the U.S. refineries, with an

---

[66] For a discussion of LCAs and biofuels, see (archived) CRS Report R40460, *Calculation of Lifecycle Greenhouse Gas Emissions for the Renewable Fuel Standard (RFS)*, by Brent D. Yacobucci and Kelsi Bracmort

[67] Greenhouse gases include carbon dioxide (CO_2), methane (CH_4), nitrous oxide (N_2O), hydrofluorocarbons (HFCs), perfluorocarbons (PFCs), and sulfur hexafluoride (SF_6), among many others. In order to compare and aggregate different greenhouse gases, various techniques have been developed to index the effect each greenhouse gas has to that of carbon dioxide, where the effect of CO_2 equals one. When the various gases are indexed and aggregated, their combined quantity is described as the CO_2-equivalent.

average range of increases from 14%-20% over the average well-to-wheel (WTW) for all transportation fuels sold or distributed in the United States; and

2. Well-to-tank (WTT) emissions, which omit the combustion phase, have an average range of increase from 72%-111% over the average WTT emissions for all transportation fuels sold or distributed in the United States.

These dramatically different ranges highlight the importance of LCA boundaries and data presentation. When a comparison is expressed on a WTT basis rather than on a WTW basis, GHG emissions from Canadian oil sands crudes show values that are significantly higher than reference crudes. This difference is due to the omission of the combustion phase, which generates the vast majority of GHG emissions and generally yields minimal variance among different crude oils.

The studies identify two main reasons for the range of increases in GHG emissions intensity:

- oil sands are heavier and more viscous than lighter crude oil types on average, and thus require more energy- and resource-intensive activities to extract; and

- oil sands are compositionally deficient in hydrogen, and have a higher carbon, sulfur, and heavy metal content than lighter crude oil types on average, and thus require more processing to yield consumable fuels by U.S. standards.

Figure 8 presents a summary of the WTW GHG emissions estimates for various Canadian oil sands crude types and production processes as reported by several studies. Variability among the estimates is the result of each study's design and input assumptions.[68]

---

[68] Discussed in detail in CRS Report R42537, *Canadian Oil Sands Life-Cycle Assessments of Greenhouse Gas Emissions*, by Richard K. Lattanzio.

Figure 8. Well-to-Wheel GHG Emissions Estimates for Canadian Oil Sands Crudes

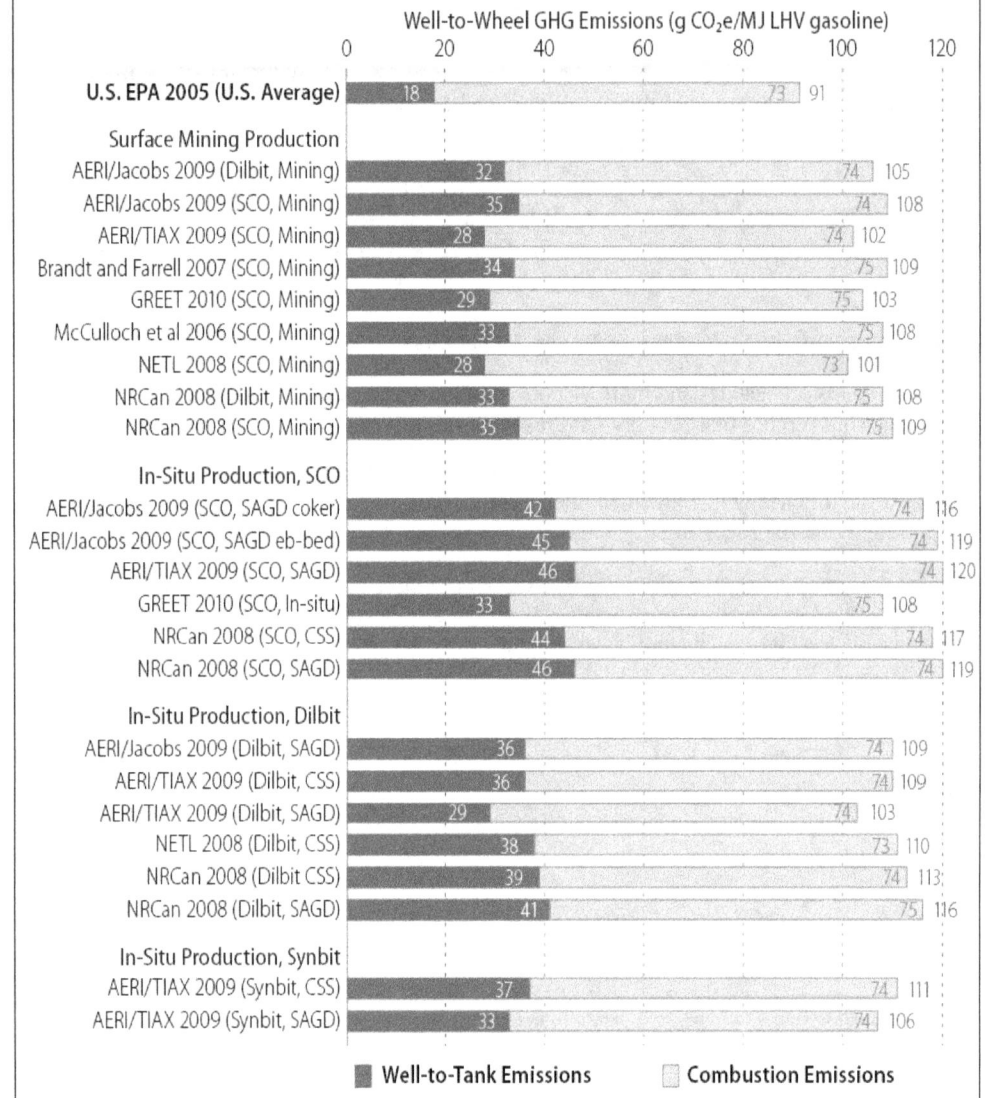

Source: CRS, from studies cited in CRS Report R42537, *Canadian Oil Sands: Life-Cycle Assessments of Greenhouse Gas Emissions*, by Richard K. Lattanzio. Average U.S. petroleum base ine for 2005 provided by U.S. Environmental Protection Agency (U.S. EPA), *Renewable Fuel Standard Program (RFS2): Regulatory Impact Analysis*, February 2010, EPA-420-R-10-006, with data sourced from DOE/NETL, *Development of Baseline Data and Analysis of Life Cycle GHG Emissions of Petroleum Based Fuels*, November 2008.

Notes: Emission intensity measured in grams of carbon dioxide-equivalent per megajoule of lower heating value gasoline (gCO2e/MJ LHV). U.S. EPA 2005 (U.S. Average) assesses "the average life cycle GHG profile for transportation fuels sold or distributed in the United States in 2005 [and] is determined based on the weighted average of fuels produced in the U.S. plus fuels imported into the U.S. minus fuels produced in the U.S. but exported to other countries for use" (NETL 2008, p. ES-5). This baseline includes Canadian oil sands, but does not include emissions from some of the most carbon-intensive imported crude oils (e.g., Venezuelan Heavy) due to modeling uncertainties (NETL 2008, p. ES-7; NETL 2009, p. ES-2). For information on crude oil types and production processes, see CRS Report R42537, *Canadian Oil Sands: Life-Cycle Assessments of Greenhouse Gas Emissions*, by Richard K. Lattanzio.

Canadian Oil Sands Compared to Other Crude Oils

Many of the LCA studies examined by DOS compared the GHG emission intensity of Canadian oil sands crude oil to other crude oils. **Figure 9** presents the results of one of the more comprehensive studies, which was prepared by the U.S. Department of Energy's National Energy Technology Laboratory (NETL) in 2009. NETL compared WTW GHG emissions of reformulated gasoline across various crude oil feedstocks. NETL concluded that WTW GHG emissions from gasoline produced from a weighted average of Canadian oil sands crudes are approximately 17% higher than that from gasoline derived from the average mix of crudes sold or distributed in the United States in 2005 (**Figure 9**). This corresponds to an increase in WTT (i.e., "production") GHG emissions of 80% over the 2005 average production emissions for imported transportation fuels to the United States (18 gCO$_2$e/MJ).

Figure 9. Well-to-Wheel GHG Emissions Estimates for Global Crude Resources

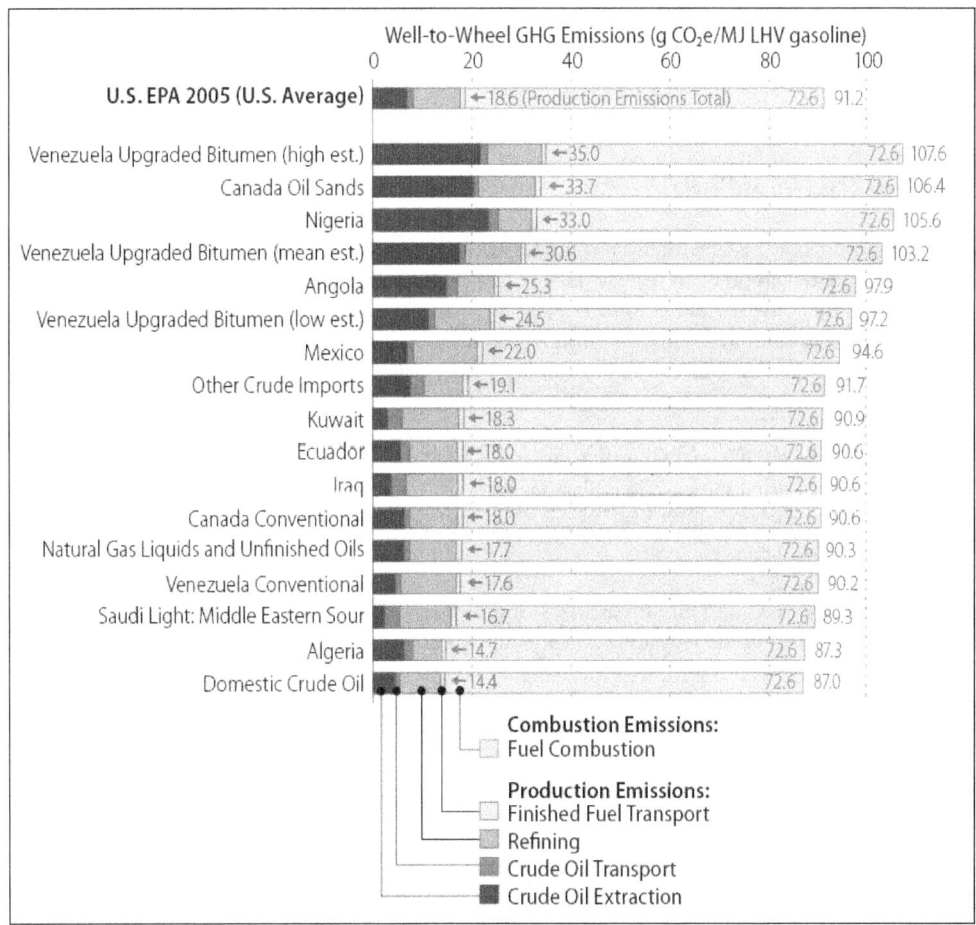

Source: CRS, from NETL, *An Evaluation of the Extraction, Transport and Refining of Imported Crude Oils and the Impact of Life Cycle Greenhouse Gas Emissions*, National Energy Technology Laboratory, March 27, 2009

Notes: For further details concerning this figure and the NETL study, see CRS Report R42537, *Canadian Oil Sands: Life-Cycle Assessments of Greenhouse Gas Emissions*, by Richard K. Lattanzio.

Similar to the LCAs of Canadian oil sands crudes, assessments of other global crude oil resources are bounded by specific design factors and input assumptions that can affect the results.[69]

Both opponents and proponents of oil sands development and the Keystone XL pipeline may be able to use results from one or more of the above studies to advance their position. For example, opponents often use WTT comparisons to highlight the GHG emissions intensity of the oil sands extraction process. On the other hand, proponents often point out that the GHG emissions intensity of oil sands is comparable to other heavy crudes that are used and/or produced in the United States. Both assertions are supported by the analyses, but the above results suggest that these assertions may not tell the complete story.

The data underlying the assertions are generated by conducting LCAs. Although LCAs have emerged as an important analytical tool for comparing the GHG emissions of various hydrocarbon resources, LCAs retain many variables and uncertainties. The life-cycle of hydrocarbon fuels is complex and differs by fuel. LCAs rely on a large number of analytical design features that are needed to model their emissions. As noted above, certain factors that could alter the results (e.g., land use changes) are omitted, due, in part, to their additional complexity. Therefore, comparing results across resources or production methods may be problematic.

Climate Change Concerns

Some groups oppose the construction of the Keystone XL pipeline because they contend it would facilitate further development of oil sands, a potential outcome that runs counter to their climate change policy objectives.[70] These objectives range from reducing the carbon intensity of the nation's fuel portfolio to reducing (or eliminating) all fossil fuel use. This range of objectives is likely related to positions concerning the severity of climate change risk and/or the need for dramatic mitigation efforts.

For example, some environmental groups are concerned that the increased imports of oil sands crudes (and the resulting increase in emissions intensity) would undermine ongoing climate mitigation efforts, such as support for less carbon-intensive energy (e.g., renewables) or energy efficiency improvements.[71]

Others have expressed more dire predictions. A prominent climate scientist, outspoken advocate, and leading opponent of the Keystone XL pipeline, James Hansen, is often quoted as saying that

---

[69] These are discussed in detail in CRS Report R42537, *Canadian Oil Sands Life-Cycle Assessments of Greenhouse Gas Emissions*, by Richard K. Lattanzio.

[70] See e.g., Kenny Bruno et al, *Tar Sands Invasion How Dirty and Expensive Oil from Canada Threatens America's New Energy Economy*, May 2010, at http://www.nrdc.org/energy/files/TarSandsInvasion.pdf

[71] See e.g., Kenny Bruno et al, *Tar Sands Invasion How Dirty and Expensive Oil from Canada Threatens America's New Energy Economy*, May 2010; Simon Mui, "Tar Sands and GHG Emissions: Setting the Record Straight," Natural Resource Defense Council Switchboard, November 16, 2010.

oil sands development would be "game over" for climate change mitigation.[72] Other advocates for stringent climate change mitigation measures repeat this phrase.[73]

A comprehensive assessment of the "game over" contention is beyond the scope of this report. The following discussion provides additional context for this notion and the broader energy/climate policy concerns voiced by pipeline opponents.

GHG Emissions Intensities of Fossil Fuels

How does the GHG emissions intensity of oil sands compare to other fossil fuels, particularly coal? Authoritative analyses that provide such comparisons are sparse. One study from a peer-review journal compares the GHG emissions intensity of oil sands with other fossil fuels. The study found that oil sands crude oil emissions intensity is slightly less than emissions intensity from underground coal mining, but surpasses the life-cycle emissions intensity from surface coal mining. **Figure 10** illustrates this result. CRS added the line with the arrows to focus one's attention on the comparison described above.

One must be cautious when singling out oil sands crudes, because other heavy crude oils would also be comparable to coal's emissions intensity, as indicated in **Figure 9**. Regardless, the relative comparison in **Figure 10** may draw the attention of certain stakeholders. If heavier crudes, such as those derived from oil sands, were to replace crude oils in the United States with less GHG emissions intensity, the emissions intensity of the U.S. energy portfolio would—all things being equal—increase. Such a result would make GHG emissions reductions more difficult.

---

[72] A more complete quote that includes this phrase: "If Canada proceeds, and we do nothing, it will be *game over* for the climate .... Canada's tar sands, deposits of sand saturated with bitumen, contain twice the amount of carbon dioxide emitted by global oil use in our entire history. If we were to fully exploit this new oil source, and continue to burn our conventional oil, gas and coal supplies, concentrations of carbon dioxide in the atmosphere eventually would reach levels higher than in the Pliocene era [emphasis added] (James Hansen, "Game Over for the Climate," *New York Times*, Op-Ed, May 9, 2012).

[73] See e.g., Interview with Bill McKibben on Bill Moyers website, February 2012, at http://billmoyers.com/2012/02/13/bill-mckibben-on-climate-change-and-the-keystone-pipeline/.

Figure 10. Life-Cycle GHG Emissions Estimates for Gasoline, Natural Gas, and Coal

GHG Emissions for Global Warming Potentials of 20 and 100 years

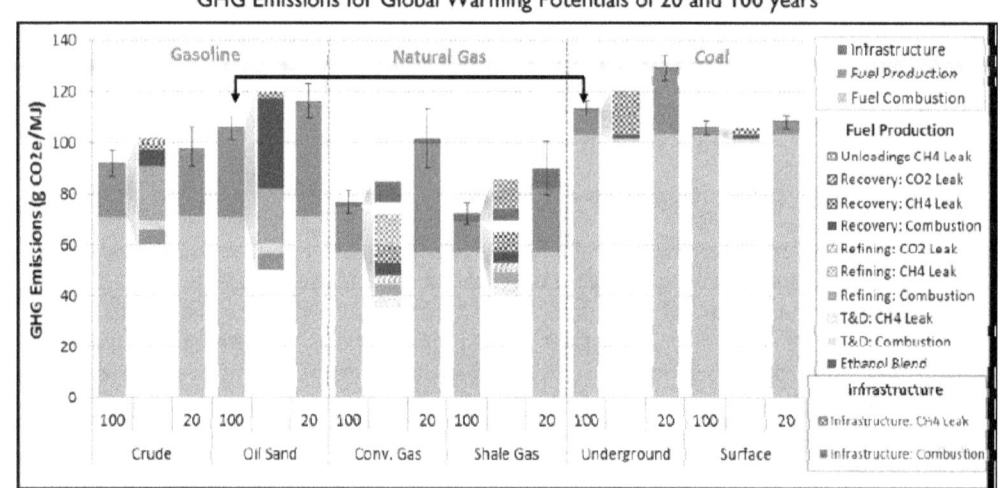

Source: Prepared by CRS from Burnham, A., et al, "Life-Cycle Greenhouse Gas Emissions of Shale Gas, Natural Gas, Coal, and Petroleum," *Environmental Science and Technology*, Vol. 46, 2012, pp. 619–627.

Notes: CRS added the line with the two arrows that connects the oil sands emission intensity with the underground coal mining emission intensity.

Fossil Fuels—Proven Reserve Comparisons

How do Alberta oil sands compare to global supplies of other fossil fuels? **Figure 11** compares the total energy that would be generated if all of the proven reserves of global fossil fuels were combusted. The data indicate that the global supply of coal's proven reserves accounts for the majority of potential energy from proven reserves of all fossil fuels. Alberta oil sands' proven reserves represent approximately 3% of the total amount of energy in global proven reserves of fossil fuels.

Readers should also use caution when examining the comparison in **Figure 11**.[74] Such a comparison is problematic for a host of reasons, an exhaustive list of which is beyond the scope of this report. In general, fossil fuels are not easily interchangeable, especially in the transportation sector. Different fuels provide different energy services, and these relationships may vary by location. For example, oil provides the energy for most of the U.S. transportation sector (e.g., motor vehicles). Altering such relationships may require dramatic infrastructure changes.

Moreover, the data in **Figure 11** do not account for the cost of extracting and developing the fossil fuel resources, which may vary by resource and location. Economic decisions are subject to technological and policy changes. For instance, a carbon constrained policy (e.g., a carbon tax) would favor natural gas over other fossil fuels—all else being equal—because natural gas emits fewer GHG emissions per unit of energy than other fossil fuels.

---

[74] Other sources have provided similar comparisons, including (1) Neil Swart and Andrew Weaver, "The Alberta Oil Sands and Climate," *Nature Climate Change*, Vol. 2, March 2012; and (2) James Hansen, "Cowards in Our Democracies: Part 2," January 2012, at http://www.columbia.edu/~jeh1/mailings/2012/20120130_CowardsPart2.pdf.

In addition, proven reserve estimates can change, as discussed above and illustrated in **Figure 3**. Ten years ago, the Alberta oil sands column in the figure below would have been absent, according to proven reserve estimates at the time. Likewise, other energy sources (e.g., gas from shale formations) have become economically feasible in recent years, altering the proven reserve calculation for natural gas.

Figure 11. Illustration of Energy from Global Fossil Fuel Sources

Based on Proven Reserve Estimates (2008)

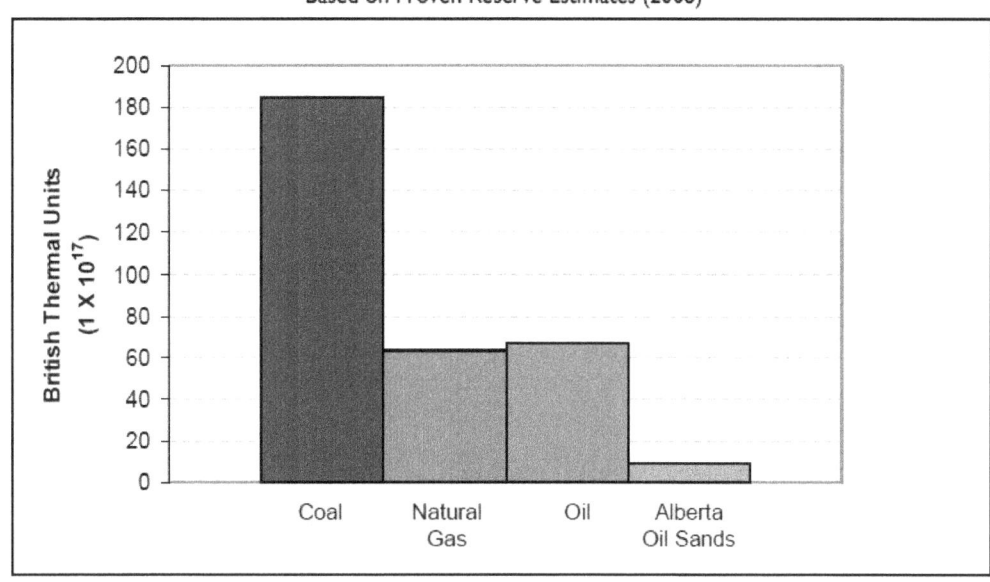

Source: Prepared by CRS; proven reserve data from Energy Information Administration (EIA), International Energy Statistics, at http://www.eia.gov. British Thermal Units generated by multiplying proven reserve data (in short tons, barrels, and cubic feet) by appropriate annual heat content data, available in EIA, *Annual Energy Review*, October 2011, Appendices.

Notes: Other comparisons of global fossil fuels can be found at (1) Neil Swart and Andrew Weaver, "The Alberta Oil Sands and C imate," *Nature Climate Change*, Vol. 2, March 2012; and (2) James Hansen, "Cowards in Our Democracies: Part 2," January 2012, at http://www.columbia.edu/~jeh1/mailings/2012/20120130_CowardsPart2.pdf.

Other Policy Decisions

The issuance of a Presidential Permit does not preclude the implementation of energy/climate policies that would support less carbon intensive fuels or encourage energy efficiency. Future policies that alter consumer behavior or affect market decisions of energy producers could counter the relative emissions intensity increase that oil sands would provide.

Oil Spills

A primary environmental concern of any oil pipeline is the risk of a spill. The impacts of an oil spill depend on multiple factors, including: the type of oil spilled and the size and location of the spill.[75] Location is generally considered the most important factor, as highlighted by DOS:

> The greatest concern would be a spill in environmentally sensitive areas, such as wetlands, flowing streams and rivers, shallow groundwater areas, areas near water intakes for drinking water or for commercial/industrial uses, and areas with populations of sensitive wildlife or plant species.[76]

Location-specific concerns played a key role in DOS's November 2011 decision to obtain additional information before making its national interest determination for TransCanada's 2008 Presidential Permit application. Regarding its decision, DOS stated:

> [P]articularly given the concentration of concerns regarding the environmental sensitivities of the current proposed route through the Sand Hills area of Nebraska, the Department has determined it needs to undertake an in-depth assessment of potential alternative routes in Nebraska.[77]

In part as a result of DOS's decision, TransCanada announced that it would work with the Nebraska Department of Environmental Quality to identify a potential pipeline route avoiding the Nebraska Sand Hills (**Table 2**).

Pipeline integrity concerns—whether real or perceived—were magnified by a 2010 oil sands crude pipeline spill in Michigan. On July 26, 2010, a 40-year old pipeline, operated by Enbridge, released approximately 800,000 gallons of oil sands crude oil[78] into Talmadge Creek, a waterway that flows into the Kalamazoo River (Michigan).[79] The National Transportation Safety Board (NTSB) issued a synopsis of its upcoming investigatory report in July 25, 2012.[80] The synopsis did not include a probable cause analysis, but it concluded that internal corrosion was not a factor in the incident.

Based on experience with pipelines historically, the Keystone XL pipeline will likely lead to some number of oil spills over the course of its operating life, regardless of design, construction, and safety measures. However, the frequency, volume, and location of spills are unknown. Some contend that proponents of the pipeline understate oil spill risks; others contend that pipeline opponents overstate the risks.

---

[75] See CRS Report RL33705, *Oil Spills in U.S. Coastal Waters Background and Governance*, by Jonathan L. Ramseur.

[76] 2011 FEIS, "Executive Summary," p. ES-9, available at http://keystonepipeline-xl.state.gov/archive/dos_docs/feis/vol1/index.htm.

[77] U.S. Department of State, "Keystone XL Pipeline Project Review Process: Decision to Seek Additional Information," Media Note, PRN 2011/1909, Office of the Spokesperson, November 10, 2011.

[78] See the Enbridge response website "Frequently Asked Questions" at http://www.response.enbridgeus.com/response/main.aspx?id=12783#Type_of_oil.; and *Tar Sands Pipelines Safety Risks* (citing a conference call with Enbridge CEO).

[79] For more up-to-date information, see EPA's Enbridge oil spill website at http://www.epa.gov/enbridgespill/index.html.

[80] See http://www.ntsb.gov/news/events/2012/marshall_mi/index.html. The final report is expected in the Fall of 2012 (personal communication with the NTSB, March 19, 2012).

A key question for policymakers is whether the Keystone XL proposed pipeline is different from other pipelines. For example, would the project impose a greater or lesser risk of an oil spill than another oil pipeline?

Oil Sands Crudes—Characteristics

Some environmental groups have argued that the pipeline would pose additional oil spill risks due to the material being transported.[81] They have asserted that diluted bitumen (Dilbit) poses particular concerns of volatility and corrosivity that may pose additional risks to the pipeline's integrity. Whether or not these issues warrant concern is debatable. Regardless, the concerns led Congress to enact provisions in P.L. 112-90 calling for further study. These issues are discussed below.

Volatility

According to a 2011 environmental groups' report, "at high temperatures, the mixture of light, gaseous condensate, and thick, heavy bitumen, can become unstable."[82] It is uncertain what constitutes a high temperature in this context. For example, would the temperature be within the range of the pipeline's operating parameters? Regardless, some have questioned this conclusion.[83]

One of the citations in the 2011 report that is cited as support for the above statement is an "expert viewpoint"[84] that does not specifically address pipeline transportation, but seems to discuss behavior of oil sands in the reservoir. The other is a study modeling liquid-column separation in oil pipelines—perhaps a relevant issue (discussed below)—but this study does not appear to distinguish between different crude oil types.[85]

Related to the assertion of volatility, the 2011 report highlights a process—described as liquid-column separation—that could potentially occur in pipelines when changes in pipeline pressure causes some of the natural gas liquid component to change into a gas bubble. According to the report, when these gas bubbles burst they release high pressure that can damage a pipeline (a process described as cavitation). The report states that "instability of DilBit can render pipelines particularly susceptible to ruptures caused by pressure spikes."[86]

However, DOS countered this assertion stating that it:

---

[81] Anthony Swift et al, *Tar Sands Pipelines Safety Risks*, Joint Report by Natural Resources Defense Council, National Wildlife Federation, Pipeline Safety Trust, and Sierra Club, February 2011 (hereafter *Tar Sands Pipelines Safety Risks*); see also Anthony Swift et al, *Pipeline and Tanker Trouble The Impact to British Columbia's Communities, Rivers, and Pacific Coastline from Tar Sands Oil Transport*, Joint Report by Natural Resources Defense Council, Pembina Institute, and Living Oceans Society, November 2011 (hereafter *Pipeline and Tanker Trouble*).

[82] *Tar Sands Pipelines Safety Risks.*

[83] See Crude Quality Inc., *Report regarding the U.S. Department of State Supplementary Draft Environmental Impact Statement*, May 2011; and Energy Resources Conservation Board, Press Release, "ERCB Addresses Statements in Natural Resources Defense Council Pipeline Safety Report," February 2011.

[84] As cited by *Tar Sands Pipelines Safety Risks*: Expert Viewpoint (John Shaw, University of Alberta) – Phase Behaviors of Heavy Oils and Bitumen," Schlumberger Ltd., 2011. The cited website no longer leads to this source, but CRS located the material using the Internet "Wayback Machine," at http://web.archive.org.

[85] Changjun Li et al., *Study on Liquid-Column Separation in Oil Transport Pipeline*, American Society of Civil Engineers, International Conference on Pipelines and Trenchless Technology 2009.

[86] *Tar Sands Pipelines Safety Risks.*

contacted the author [that NRDC cited to support the above statement]… to address this concern and determined that it would not be valid to infer from this research that dilbits are any more or less stable than other crude oils, or that they are more likely to cause pressure spikes during transport in pipelines or otherwise pose an increased risk to pipeline safety.[87]

Corrosivity

Some argue that DilBit pipelines may be more likely to fail than other crude oil pipelines because the bitumen mixtures they carry are "significantly more corrosive to pipeline systems than conventional crude."[88] Three DilBit properties of particular interest are acidity, sulfur content, and solids content, all of which may influence the overall corrosiveness of a given blend of crude oil. The 2011 report also focuses on these specific DilBit properties and their potential influence on pipeline corrosion, asserting:

> Compared to "conventional" crudes, DilBit blends are thicker and more acidic, and contain more sulfur, chloride salts, and quartz sand particles. These characteristics create a "combination of chemical corrosion and physical abrasion [that] can dramatically increase the rate of pipeline deterioration."[89]

To what extent these claims may be correct is the subject of debate. Alberta's Energy Resources Conservation Board (ERCB), among other stakeholders, has rejected the claims from the 2011 report, stating that "there is no reason to expect this product to behave in any substantially different way than other oil...."[90] Additional background on the specific DilBit characteristics of concern may offer a greater understanding of the corrosion mechanisms at issue, but not necessarily resolve the debate.

Total Acid Number

As indicated in **Table 1** (above) Canadian DilBit total acid numbers (TANs) range between 0.92 to 2.49. This range is generally higher than lighter crude oils, but comparable with other heavy oils. It is well-established that the presence of naphthenic acids in high TAN crudes can considerably increase corrosion potential in the parts of refinery distillation units operating at high temperature—above 400°F.[91] However, pipeline transportation of DilBit is expected to occur at much lower temperatures: the maximum operating temperature for Keystone XL is 150°F. Moreover, DilBit pipeline corrosion rates may not have a direct correlation with TAN values. There is evidence of more than 1,000 napthenic acid varieties with varying corrosivity, which may comprise a single TAN number.[92] TAN values depend upon the specific content and types of

---

[87] 2011 FEIS, "Potential Releases," p. 3-13.45, available at http://keystonepipeline-xl.state.gov/archive/dos_docs/feis/vol2/env/index.htm.

[88] *Tar Sands Pipelines Safety Risks.*

[89] *Tar Sands Pipelines Safety Risks.*

[90] Canadian Energy Resources Conservation Board (ERCB), "ERCB Addresses Statements in Natural Resources Defense Council Pipeline Safety Report," Press release, Calgary, Alberta, February 16, 2011.

[91] Dennis Haynes, *Naphthenic Acid Bearing Refinery Feedstocks and Corrosion Abatement*, Presentation to the AIChE Chicago Symposium, 2006, p. 7; Bruce Randolph, James Scinta, Eric Vetters, et al., *Challenges in Processing Canadian Oilsands Crude – A US Refiners' Perspective*, Canadian Crude Quality Technical Association, June 25, 2008.

[92] See Anne Shafizadeh et al., "High Acid Crudes," Presentation to the Crude Oil Quality Group New Orleans Meeting, January 30, 2003, http://www.coqa-inc.org/20030130High%20Acid%20Crudes.pdf.

---

compounds in specific crudes—which may vary significantly from crude to crude.[93] Some testing of pipeline steels has shown that Canadian oil sands crudes exhibit "very low corrosion rates" despite high TAN numbers, in part because they contain other "inhibitor" compounds that reduce the corrosivity of the bitumen.[94] Therefore, it is uncertain whether refiners' experiences with corrosion from high TAN crudes can be directly extended to DilBit transmission pipelines.

Sulfur Content

Another factor in crude oil corrosivity is sulfur content. Crude oils sent to U.S. refineries typically contain 0.5% to 2.5% sulfur.[95] As indicated in **Table 1**, DilBits have sulfur content substantially above this range—between 3% and 5%. In sour crudes (> 1% sulfur content), sulfur is present as hydrogen sulfide (H_2S),[96] which can combine with water to form sulfuric acid (H_2SO_4), a strongly corrosive acid. Like napthenic acid corrosion (discussed above), sulfidic corrosion is a high temperature phenomenon, beginning above 500°F.[97] In pipelines, H_2S can also interact with napthenic acids, carbon dioxide (CO_2) and solids, complicating the possible corrosion processes at work. Research and refiner experience suggest that sulfuric and napthenic acid corrosivity can be inhibited or augmented by the presence of specific sulfur compounds depending upon the chemical characteristics of those compounds (e.g., how readily they decompose into H_2S), whether they are in liquid or vapor phase, and other factors.[98] In some cases, H_2S can form a protective sulfide coating that actually prevents corrosion.[99] Thus, as in the case of TAN levels, sulfur content in crude oil may not accurately reflect corrosivity, notwithstanding the common use of sulfur content to indicate sulfidic corrosion potential in refinery equipment.[100] For these reasons, the direct application of sulfidic corrosion experience in refineries to lower temperature crude oil pipelines may be inconsistent with chemical processes involved.

---

[93] Canadian Crude Quality Technical Association, TAN Phase III Project, Meeting Minutes of June 23, 2009, http://www.ccqta.com/docs/documents/Projects/TAN_Phase_III/TAN%20Phase%20III%20March%202009%20Minutes.pdf.

[94] Rena Liviniuk, et al., "Organic Acid Structure – A Correlation With Corrosivity," AM-09-20, Presented to the National Petrochemical and Refiners Association, Annual Meeting, March 22-24, 2009, San Antonio, TX, p. 9.

[95] U.S. Energy Information Administration, "Crude Oil Input Qualities: Sulfur Content, Annual," Internet table, June 29, 2011, http://www.eia.gov/dnav/pet/pet_pnp_crq_a_EPC0_YCS_pct_a.htm.

[96] H_2S is generated at temperatures greater than 392 F (200 C) through a reaction between carbon-containing and sulfur-containing compounds in the crude. Thus, H_2S can be generated during the oil sands thermal extraction process. See: G.G. Hoffmann, et al., "Thermal Recovery Processes and Hydrogen Sulfide Formation," Presented at the Society of Petroleum Engineers International Symposium on Oilfield Chemistry, San Antonio, Texas, February 14-17, 1995.

[97] H.M. Shalaby, "Refining of Kuwait's Heavy Crude Oil: Materials Challenges," Workshop on Corrosion and Protection of Metals, Arab School for Science and Technology, Kuwait, December 3-7, 2005, p. 5; http://www.arabschool.org/pdf_notes/20_REFINING_OF_KUWAITS_HEAVY_CRUDE_OIL.pdf.

[98] Ibid., p.6; Heather Dettman, et al, "Refinery Corrosion: The Influence of Organic Acid and Sulphur Compund Structure on Global Crude Corrosivity," Presentation to the 5th NCUT Upgrading and Refining Conference 2009, Edmonton, Alberta, September 14 - 16, 2009; Dennis Haynes, 2006, p. 8.

[99] Gregory R. Ruschau, and Mohammed A. Al-Anez, *Oil and Gas Exploration and Production*, Appendix S, Corrosion Prevention, p. S6, in: CC Technologies Laboratories, Inc., *Corrosion Costs And Preventive Strategies In The United States*, Report to the U.S. Federal Highway Administration, Office of Infrastructure Research and Development, Report FHWA-RD-01-156, September 2001, http://www.corrosioncost.com/pdf/oilgas.pdf.

[100] H.M Shalaby, 2005, p. 6.

Abrasive Solids

Solids suspended in crude oil have the potential to accelerate corrosion in pipelines either by settling out (forming corrosive conditions beneath them) or through abrasion. Abrasion has been raised as a particular concern for DilBit pipelines because DilBit may contain significantly more solids than conventional crudes.[101] These solids, it is argued, might wear away the interior walls of a pipeline and exacerbate wall loss from acidic corrosion. Some have compared this process to sandblasters.[102] However, CRS is not aware of publically available research that has examined whether the conditions exist for significant internal abrasion of DilBit pipelines. Crude oils with high solids content are also generally filtered to meet the quality specifications set by pipelines and refiners. Thus DilBit blends may have solids content higher than other types of crudes, but still within an acceptable range for pipeline and refinery operations.

Keystone XL Pipeline Operating Parameters

Multiple parties submitted comments to DOS, highlighting the Keystone XL pipeline operating parameters as a particular concern.[103] The 2011 environmental groups' report claims that "the risks of corrosion and the abrasive nature of DilBit are made worse by the relatively high heat and pressure."[104]

The report asserts the pipeline will be operating at temperatures "up to 158° F," which is substantially higher than conventional crude pipelines, which, according to the report, operate at less than 100° F.[105] TransCanada has stated that "oil in a line like this comes into our pipeline between 80-120°F, and it stays within that temperature range during transport."[106] In the 2011 FEIS, DOS states that the maximum operating temperature of the proposed pipeline would not exceed 150° F. It is uncertain whether this 150° F mark is an upper bound that might be approached on rare occasions, or whether the operating temperature would typically hover near this maximum. Either way, it is below the maximum operational temperature cited by some environmental groups.

According to the report, conventional crude pipeline pressure is 600 pounds per square-inch (PSI), while diluted bitumen requires a pipeline pressure of 1,440 psi[107] A subsequent 2011 report lists this figure as 2,130 psi.[108] Regardless, the 2011 FEIS lists the Keystone XL operating pressure as 1,308 psi.

---

[101] Baker Hughes Inc., *Planning Ahead for Effective Canadian Crude Processing*, Sugar Land, TX, 2010, p. 4, http://www.bakerhughes.com/assets/media/whitepapers/4c2a3c8ffa7e1c3c7400001d/file/28271-canadian_crudeoil_update_whitepaper_06-10.pdf.pdf&fs=1497549.

[102] *Tar Sands Pipelines Safety Risks.*.

[103] See 2011 final EIS, "Appendix A, Responses to Comments and Scoping Summary Report," available at http://keystonepipeline-xl.state.gov/archive/dos_docs/feis/vol3and4/appendixa/index.htm.

[104] *Tar Sands Pipelines Safety Risks.*

[105] *Tar Sands Pipelines Safety Risks.*

[106] TransCanada, "TransCanada's Keystone XL Pipeline – Know the Facts," fact sheet, May 2011, http://www.transcanada.com/docs/Key_Projects/know_the_facts_kxl.pdf.

[107] *Tar Sands Pipelines Safety Risks.*

[108] *Pipeline and Tanker Trouble.*

The degree to which the Keystone XL pipeline's operating parameters differ from other oil pipeline operating parameters is beyond the scope of this report. In general, the Keystone XL operating parameters are different, because diluted bitumen (and heavy crude oils) are more viscous (resistant to flow) than conventional crude oil. According to a 2011 review of heavy crude transportation:

> Pipelining of heavy oil presents problems like instability of asphaltenes, paraffin precipitation and high viscosity that cause multiphase flow, clogging of pipes, high-pressure drops, and production stops.[109]

The same review describes several options that may be used "to resolve or improve pipelining of heavy and extra-heavy crude oil." These options include dilution with other substances and increasing/conserving the oil's temperature. Both of these options would reduce viscosity and both seem to be part of the Keystone XL proposed operations.

DOS states that the proposed pipeline would satisfy the Department of Transportation's Pipeline and Hazardous Materials Safety Administration (PHMSA) regulations (49 CFR Part 195) that apply to hazardous liquid pipelines. In addition, Keystone agreed to implement 57 additional measures developed by PHMSA. In consultation with PHMSA, DOS determined that incorporation of those conditions:

> would result in a Project that would have a degree of safety over any other typically constructed domestic oil pipeline system under current code and a degree of safety along the entire length of the pipeline system similar to that which is required in High Consequence Areas (HCAs) as defined in 49 CFR 195.450.[110]

The *degree* to which the additional 57 measures mitigate risk is debatable. For instance, the primary author of the 2011 environmental groups' report argued that only 12 of these conditions actually differ in some way from minimum requirements.[111]

Oil Pipeline Spill Data from Alberta

Many stakeholders have argued a comparison of oil spill data from Alberta and the United States indicates that internal corrosion has led to substantially more oil spills in the Alberta pipeline system than the U.S. system.[112] They reason that this difference is likely related to high proportion of oil sands crudes, which have been in the Alberta system since the 1980s. In contrast, the first dedicated oil sands crudes pipeline in the United States, the Alberta Clipper, began operating in 2010.[113]

DOS rejected this assertion, stating:

---

[109] Rafael Martinez-Palou et al., "Transportation of Heavy and Extra-Heavy Crude Oil by Pipeline: A Review," *Journal of Petroleum Science and Engineering*, Vol. 75, pp. 274-282, January 2011.

[110] 2011 FEIS, "Project Description," p. 2-23, available at http://keystonepipeline-xl.state.gov/archive/dos_docs/feis/vol1/index.htm.

[111] Anthony Swift, "Clinton's Tar Sands Pipeline 'Safety Conditions' are Smoke and Mirrors," August 19, 2011, at http://switchboard.nrdc.org.

[112] 2011 FEIS, Appendix A (see footnote 59).

[113] *Tar Sands Pipelines Safety Risks.*

> [T]here is no evidence that the transportation of oil sands derived crude oil in Alberta has resulted in a higher corrosion related failure rate than occurs in the transportation of the variable-sourced crude oils in the U.S. system.[114]

Further, DOS pointed out that a comparison of the oil spill data is problematic for various reasons. In particular, the scopes of the data collected in each nation are different. Canadian data includes smaller spills and spills from certain pipelines not covered by PHMSA regulations. To address these discrepancies in data collection, PHMSA prepared a comparison of pipeline incidents of similar scopes between the two databases. This comparison was part of the 2011 FEIS and is provided below in **Table 4**.

Table 4. PHMSA Comparison of Oil Pipeline Incidents in Alberta and United States

2002 - 2010

Crude Oil Pipeline Failures U.S. and Alberta \ (2002-2010)		
U.S. Crude Oil Pipeline Incident Historya		
Incident/Failure Case	Failures/Year	Failures per 1,000 Pipeline Miles per Year
Corrosion - External	9.8	0.19
Corrosion - Internal	22.1	0.42
All Failures	89.3	1.70
Alberta Crude Oil Pipeline Incident Historyb		
Corrosion - External	2.3	0.21
Corrosion - Internal	3.6	0.32
All Failures	22.0	1.97

Source: Reproduced by CRS; original table from 2011 FEIS, , p. 3.13-38 (Table 3.13.5-4).

Notes: The following notes are included in the table in the 2011 FEIS:

a. PHMSA includes spill incidents greater than 5 gallons. U.S. had 52,475 miles of crude oil pipe ines in 2008.

b. Alberta Energy and Utility Board Report, includes spills greater than and less than 5 bbls. Alberta had 11,187 miles of crude oil pipelines in 2006.

This comparison indicates that internal corrosion failures (per 1,000 miles of pipeline) were approximately 30% higher in the U.S. system (0.42 vs. 0.32). Regardless, such comparisons are challenging, if not impossible, considering the range of potential factors—pipeline age, enforcement, etc.—that may affect the underlying data. For this reason, the above comparison might be described as preliminary.

Keystone XL Spill Frequency Estimates

Spill frequency estimates for the Keystone XL project have been a subject of debate. During the NEPA process, Keystone submitted a spill frequency estimate of 0.22 spills per year. The company derived this estimate by using historical databases from PHMSA and then applying

---

[114] 2011 FEIS, "Potential Releases," p. 3.13-38 (see footnote 87).

project-specific factors, such as regulatory requirements, material strength, and technological advances.

However, some questioned Keystone's modified estimate, arguing that the pipeline's operating parameters—temperatures and pressures higher than conventional crude pipelines—would yield spill frequencies above historical averages, rather than below.[115]

Subsequent to Keystone's estimate, the DOS estimated that a spill over 50 barrels would occur between 1.2 to 1.8 times per year; spills of any size would occur between 1.8 to 2.5 times per year.[116]

Another potential source of data is the pipeline operating history of Keystone. Keystone has operated the Keystone Mainline pipeline and the Cushing Extension since 2010. Since that time the Keystone pipeline has generated 14 unintentional releases. DOS cites personal communication with PHMSA staff, who stated that these incidents are "not unusual start-up issues that occur on pipeline and are not unique."[117] Regardless, this figure is considerably higher than the Keystone XL spill frequency estimates DOS included in its 2011 FEIS.

Spill Size Estimates

Citing the PHMSA significant incident database,[118] DOS indicates that between 1990 and 2010, the average spill size for onshore hazardous liquid pipelines, which includes both oil and other materials, was less than 1,000 barrels (42,000 gallons).[119] Using this database, CRS calculated the exact average spill to be 918 barrels (38,556 gallons). Per the spill size classification included in the 2011 FEIS, the average spill would be considered a "large spill."[120]

One may question whether this database is the best tool for predicting spill size from the Keystone XL pipeline. The database includes oil and other hazardous liquids; pipelines of varying sizes and pressures; and pipelines of varying ages. A more refined comparison may offer policymakers a better prediction of possible spill size, but the PHMSA database is not immediately amenable to a more tailored assessment.

In its 2011 FEIS, DOS seems to suggest that "very large spills" (defined as greater than 5,000 barrels or 210,000 gallons) would require a dramatic event. According to DOS:

> A very large spill from the pipeline would likely require the occurrence of an event that would shear the pipeline such as major earth movement resulting from slides, major earth movement resulting from an earthquake, major flood flows eroding river banks at non-HDD

---

[115] See John Stansbury, *Analysis of Frequency, Magnitude and Consequence of Worst-Case Spills from the Proposed Keystone XL Pipeline,* Submitted as a comment to the supplemental draft EIS and later cited in the 2011 FEIS.

[116] 2011 FEIS, "Potential Releases," pp. 3.13-18 – 3.13-21 (see footnote 87).

[117] 2011 FEIS, "Potential Releases," p. 3.13-11 (see footnote 87).

[118] The significant incident database represents a subset of all incidents. To qualify as "significant" an incident must result in one of the following: (1) a fatality or injury requiring in-patient hospitalization; (2) $50,000 or more in total costs, measured in 1984 dollars; (3) a highly volatile liquid release of 5 barrels or more or other liquid releases of 50 barrels or more; or (4) a liquid releases resulting in an unintentional fire or explosion.

[119] 2011 FEIS, "Potential Releases," p. 3.13-15 (see footnote 87).

[120] Ibid.

crossings, mechanical damage from third-party excavation or drilling work, or vandalism, sabotage, or terrorist actions.[121]

This assertion will be tested when the NTSB releases its investigation results for the July 2010 Enbridge oil spill.[122] That spill was a "very large spill," releasing over 800,000 gallons into the Kalamazoo River in Michigan.

Regardless, an average spill can require substantial cleanup efforts in certain locations. The July 2011 ExxonMobil spill into the Yellowstone River was approximately 42,000 gallons. The EPA is overseeing this oil spill response. In August 2011, over 1,000 personnel were engaged in cleanup and shoreline assessment efforts.[123] As of February 2012, the federal government has assigned $3.8 million from the Oil Spill Liability Trust Fund to address response activities.[124] This figure would not capture the expenses from the responsible party.

Environmental Impacts of Spills of Oil Sands Crude

Some contend that the distinct chemical composition of oil sands crude (e.g., DilBit) would pose a greater environmental risk from an oil spill than other crudes.[125] CRS is not aware of an authoritative study that has examined this assertion. Although parallels may be drawn between the possible behavior of conventional crudes and DilBit, studies are scarce regarding spills of heavy crudes with the specific composition of Canadian heavy crudes.

The behavior of crude oil spills and the fate of crude oil in the subsurface have been studied extensively around the world for a wide range of conventional crudes and other petrochemicals in both experimental settings and actual spills (e.g., Bemidji, Minnesota in 1979).[126] These include studies of specific chemical components that may be present in DilBit (e.g., benzene).[127] Based on extensive experience with other crudes and DilBit constituents, analysts may claim

---

[121] Ibid.

[122] Although a synopsis of this report was made available July 10, 2012, NTSB has not released the final report. See http://www.ntsb.gov/news/events/2012/marshall_mi/index.html.

[123] See EPA Update on Yellowstone River Oil Spill (Silvertip Pipeline), August 12, 2011, at http://www.epa.gov/yellowstoneriverspill/.

[124] Personal communication with U.S. Coast Guard, February 14, 2012.

[125] Swift et al, p. 7.

[126] See, for example, work compiled by the U.S. Geological Survey about the 1979 crude oil spill near Bemidji, MN, which contaminated a shallow aquifer: U.S. Geological Survey, "Crude Oil Contamination in the Shallow Subsurface: Bemidji, Minnesota," Internet page, July 20, 2011, http://toxics.usgs.gov/sites/bemidji_page.html. See also: M. Whittaker, S.J.T. Pollard, and T.E. Fallick, "Characterisation of Refractory Wastes at Heavy Oil-Contaminated Sites: A Review of Conventional and Novel Analytical Methods," *Environmental Technology*, Vol. 16, No. 11, November 1, 1995, pp. 1009-1033; S Khaitan et al., "Remediation of Sites Contaminated by Oil Refinery Operations," *Environmental Progress*, Vol. 25, No. 1, April 2006, pp. 20-31.

[127] See, for example: Lisa M. Geig et al., "Intrinsic Bioremediation of Petroleum Hydrocarbons in a Gas Condensate-Contaminated Aquifer," *Environmental Science and Technology*, vol. 33, no. 15 (1999), pp. 2550-2560; Paul E. Hardisty, et al., "Characterization of LNAPL in Fractured Rock," *Quarterly Journal of Engineering Geology & Hydrogeology*, Vol. 36, No. 4, November 2003, p. 343-354; J.L. Busch-Harris, e al., "In Situ Assessment of Benzene Biodegradation Potential in a Gas Condensate Contaminated Aquifer," Proceedings of 11th Annual International Petroleum Environmental Conference, Albuquerque, NM, October 12-15, 2004; John A. Connor, et al., "Nature, Frequency, and Cost of Environmental Remediation at Onshore Oil and Gas Exploration and Production Sites," *Remediation*, Vol. 21, No. 3, Summer 2011, pp. 121-144; Bruce E Rittmann, et al., *Natural Attenuation for Groundwater Remediation*, National Academy Press, 2000.

---

considerable confidence in models of DilBit behavior around groundwater. For example, the Energy Resources Conservation Board has stated that "DilBit should behave in much the same manner as other crude oils of similar characteristics.[128]

All spilled oil begins to "weather" or separate into different components over time. In general, heavier oils, like DilBit, are more persistent and may present greater technical challenges in oil removal operations than lighter crude oils. For a land spill, the heavier and more viscous components (i.e., the asphaltenes) would likely remain trapped in soil pores above the water table. It is also likely that the lighter constituents would partly evaporate and not be transported down through the soil with the heavier components.

However, if an oil spill reached the water table, some of the more soluble portions would likely dissolve into the groundwater and be transported in the direction of regional groundwater flow. The ultimate extent, shape, and composition of a groundwater contaminant plume resulting from a DilBit spill would depend on the specific characteristics of the soil, aquifer, and the amount and duration of the accidental release.

The heavier components of a DilBit spill would be difficult to remove from the soil during cleanup operations, and may require wholesale soil removal instead of other remediation techniques.[129] These challenges may come at a higher cost. In an oil spill model prepared for EPA, the model estimates that spills of heavy oil will cost nearly twice as much to clean up as comparable spills of conventional crude oil.[130]

Crude oils may contain multiple compounds that present toxicity concerns. DOS stated that "based on the combination of toxicity, solubility, and bioavailability, benzene was determined to dominate toxicity associated with potential crude oil spills."[131] Benzene and other BTEX compounds (benzene, toluene, ethyl benzene, and xylene) are generally in greater proportions in the lighter crude oils and particularly in refined products like gasoline.[132] In its 2011 FEIS, DOS compared the BTEX content of crude oil derived from oil sands (DilBit and DilSynBit) with conventional crude oils from Canada. The BTEX content of oil sands crudes ranged from 5,800 parts per million (ppm) to 9,100 ppm. The BTEX contents of conventional crude oils ranged from 5,800 ppm to 29,100 ppm.[133]

Other toxic compounds of concern in crude oils are polycyclic aromatic hydrocarbons (PAHs). Generally, PAHs are more toxic than BTEX and evaporate at a slower rate, but they are less soluble in water. The National Research Council's *Oil in the Sea* report stated that with

---

[128] Canadian Energy Resources Conservation Board (ERCB), "ERCB Addresses Statements in Natural Resources Defense Council Pipeline Safety Report," Press release, Calgary, Alberta, February 16, 2011.

[129] One such other method is "pump and treat," which involves cleaning soil and groundwater contamination by pumping and capturing the contaminated groundwater, then treating it at the surface to remove the contaminants. The same technique may be used to extract soil gas vapor from contaminated soil above the water table. For more information, see Environmental Protection Agency, *Basics of Pump-and-Treat Ground-Water Remediation Technology*, EPA/800/8-90003, March 1990.

[130] Dagmar Etkin, *Modeling Oil Spill Response and Damages Costs*, Proceedings of the 5th Biennial Freshwater Spills Symposium, 2004, at http://www.environmental-research.com.

[131] 2011 FEIS, "Potential Releases," p. 3.13-80 (see footnote 87).

[132] For a comprehensive discussion, see National Research Council, *Oil in the Sea III Inputs, Fates, and Effects*, National Academies of Science, February 2003.

[133] 2011 FEIS, "Potential Releases," Table 3.13.5-6, p. 3.13-45 (see footnote 87).

weathering/evaporation and the resulting loss of BTEX, PAHs become more important contributors to the remaining oil's toxicity.[134]

Unlike BTEX, the 2011 FEIS does not include a comparison of PAH concentrations across different crude oils. DOS states that PAH concentrations of crude oils that would be transported in the Keystone XL pipeline are unknown, because this information is proprietary.[135] Some commenters, including EPA, took issue with this during the EIS review process.[136]

Heavy metals may also be a concern. A 2011 NRDC report states that Dilbit contains quantities of heavy metals, particularly vanadium and nickel, that are "significantly larger" than conventional crude oil.[137] Assuming conventional oil means lighter crudes, this statement is largely correct.[138] However, the heavy metal concentrations in DilBit are similar to some other heavy crude oils, such as Mexican and Venezuela crudes that are processed in Gulf Coast refineries.[139] Most, if not all, of this crude oil arrives in the United States via vessel.[140]

Further Study

DOT officials acknowledge that they have not performed any specific studies nor reassessments of pipeline safety risks that might be unique to DilBit.[141] In addition, DOS points out that "a focused, peer-reviewed study of the potential corrosivity/erosivity of WCSB oil sands derived crude oils relative to other crude oils has not yet been conducted."[142]

Some in Congress have called for a review of DOT pipeline safety regulations to determine whether new regulations for Canadian heavy crudes are needed to account for any unique properties they may have. Accordingly, P.L. 112-90 requires PHMSA to review whether current regulations are sufficient to regulate pipelines transmitting "diluted bitumen," and analyze whether such oil presents an increased risk of release (§16).

Oil Sands Extraction Concerns

Opponents of the Keystone XL pipeline and oil sands development often highlight the environmental impacts that pertain to the region in which the oil sands resources are extracted. In general, these local/regional impacts from Canadian oil sands development may not directly

---

[134] National Research Council, 2003, p. 126.

[135] 2011 FEIS, "Potential Releases," p. 3.13-31 (see footnote 87).

[136] See footnote 57 regarding EPA's June 6, 2011 comments.

[137] Anthony Swift, Susan Casey-Lefkowitz, and Elizabeth Shope, *Tar Sands Pipelines Safety Risks*, Natural Resources Defense Council (NRDC), February 2011.

[138] Based on a comparison of crude oil assays from sources listed in Table 1.

[139] 2011 FEIS, "Potential Releases," Table 3.13.5-7 (see footnote 87).

[140] Although a considerable percentage of oil imports come from Mexico (e.g., approximately 12% of crude oil imports in 2010), the EIA states that "Mexico does not have any international pipeline connections, with most exports leaving the country via tanker from three export terminals in the southern part of the country." EIA, Country Analysis Briefs, at http://www.eia.gov/cabs/Mexico/Full.html.

[141] The Honorable Cynthia L. Quarterman, Administrator, Pipeline and Hazardous Materials Safety Administration, U.S. Department of Transportation, Testimony before the U.S. House Committee on Energy and Commerce, Subcommittee on Energy and Power, Hearing on "The American Energy Initiative," June 16, 2011.

[142] 2011 FEIS, "Potential Releases," p. 3.13-43 (see footnote 87).

affect public health or the environment in the United States. DOS points out that, pursuant to NEPA or applicable Executive Orders, it is not required to analyze the environment or activities outside of the United States (see "Consideration of Environmental Impacts Outside of the United States"). Still, pursuant to DOS policy and in response to concerns that the proposed project "would contribute to certain continental scale environmental impact,"[143] DOS included a summary of information regarding environmental analyses and regulations related to the Canadian portion of the proposed Keystone XL Project and WCSB oil sands production. This inclusion reflects the level of interest these issues have received in recent years.

The scope and degree of the extraction-related impacts is a subject of some debate. A comprehensive assessment of extraction-related concerns is beyond the scope of this report.[144] The following sections include discussions of two selected topics: land disturbance and water resource issues.

Land Disturbances

Both oil sands mining and in situ operations disturb the surrounding land to some degree. Land disturbances from mining operations include:

- clearance and excavation of a relatively large surface area,

- storage of removed overburden (e.g., vegetation soil), and

- construction of tailings ponds to contain extraction process wastestreams.

Many stakeholders associate in situ operations with "minimal land disturbances."[145] However, some research suggests the comparison between the two processes is more complicated. A 2009 study described the different impacts from the two processes in the following manner:

> Surface mining and in situ recovery affect the landscape in different ways. Land use of surface mining is comprised largely of polygonal features (mine sites, overburden storage, tailing ponds and end pit lakes); whereas in situ development is mostly defined by linear features that extend across the lease area (networks of seismic lines, access roads, pipelines and well sites).[146]

Although the actual extraction site at in situ operations impacts substantially less land than at mining sites, some contend that in situ processes may ultimately create a larger disturbance, because the dispersed nature of in situ operations increases landscape fragmentation.[147] In addition, one study finds that in situ operations disturb more land (per unit of oil) than mining,

---

[143] 2011 FEIS, "Cumulative Impacts" section, p. 3.14-61 available at http://keystonepipeline-xl.state.gov/archive/dos_docs/feis/vol2/env/index.htm.

[144] Perhaps the most comprehensive assessment of potential environmental concerns was prepared by the Royal Society of Canada. See P. Gosselin et al., *Environmental and Health Impacts of Canada's Oil Sands Industry*, The Royal Society of Canada, Expert Panel Report, Ottawa, Ontario, December 15, 2010.

[145] P. Gosselin et al., *Environmental and Health Impacts of Canada's Oil Sands Industry*, The Royal Society of Canada, Expert Panel Report, Ottawa, Ontario, December 15, 2010.

[146] Sarah M Jordaan et al, "Quantifying Land Use of Oil Sands Production: a Life Cycle Perspective," *Environmental Research Letters*, 2009.

[147] See e.g., Dan Woynillowicz et al, *Oil Sands Fever*, Pembina Institute, 2005; Pembina Institute, Mining vs. In Situ: Factsheet, 2012; Sarah M Jordaan et al, "Quantifying Land Use of Oil Sands Production: a Life Cycle Perspective," *Environmental Research Letters*, 2009.

---

when natural gas requirements are considered.[148] As noted above, in situ operations require energy (i.e., natural gas) to generate the steam needed to extract the underlying resource. According to the study, the land disturbances from the natural gas development contribute a major portion of in situ's total land disturbance.

How does land disturbance from oil sands operations compare to conventional oil development? Almost all forms of energy production disturb the land to some degree. A 2010 study compared land disturbances from Alberta oil sands operations with conventional oil development in Alberta and California.[149] **Figure 12** illustrates the results. The figure indicates that in situ oil sands operations have a substantially higher energy yield—energy produced per disturbed land (measured in petajoules per hectare)—than other sources. However, when natural gas use is included in the estimate, in situ operations' energy yield decreases substantially, making its energy yield equivalent to California oil, but still greater than mining operations in Canada.[150] The Alberta Chamber of Resources estimates that in situ production requires approximately four times the quantity of natural gas used for surface mining on a production volume basis.[151] Therefore, the factor of natural gas plays an important role in energy yield estimates.

Figure 12. Illustrative Comparison of Energy Yields by Selected Sources

Energy Produced per Amount of Disturbed Land

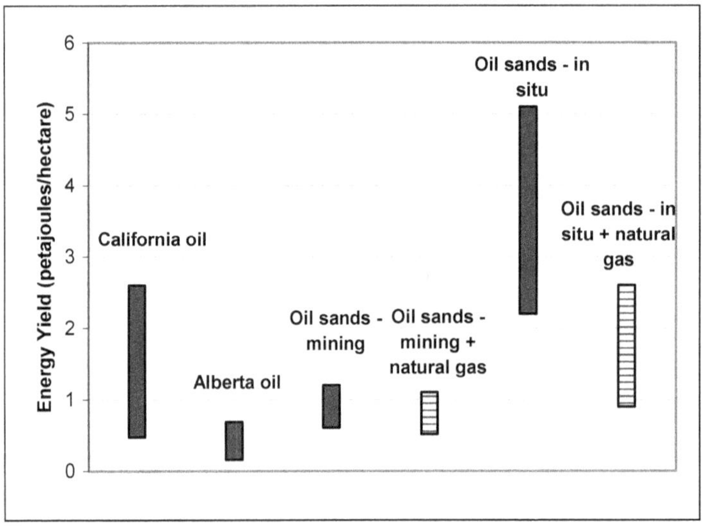

Source: Prepared by CRS; data from Sonia Yeh et al, "Land Use Greenhouse Gas Emissions from Conventional Oil Production and Oil Sands," *Environmental Science and Technology*, 44(22): 8766-8722, 2010.

Notes: Columns reflect the range of values reported by Yeh, 2010. In the main text of the 2010 study, the authors exclude the natural gas components of oil sands mining and in situ operations (represented above by the

---

[148] Sarah M Jordaan et al, "Quantifying Land Use of Oil Sands Production: a Life Cycle Perspective," *Environmental Research Letters*, 2009.

[149] Sonia Yeh et al, "Land Use Greenhouse Gas Emissions from Conventional Oil Production and Oil Sands," *Environmental Science and Technology*, 44(22): 8766-8722, 2010.

[150] In the main text of the 2010 study (Yeh et al), the authors exclude the natural gas components of oil sands mining and in situ operations (represented above by the striped columns), but provide the data in supplementary information.

[151] Alberta Chamber of Resources, *Oil Sands Technology Roadmap*, 2004.

striped columns), but provide the data in supplementary information. Including the natural gas component lowers the energy yield. Such a component was not part of the conventional Caifornia and Aberta oil data.

Another factor in land disturbance assessments is the type of land disturbed. The Alberta oil sands are located within Canada's boreal forest, a large area that contains 35% of the world's wetlands. The forest's ecosystems support a wide range of biodiversity and provide key ecological services. For example, the boreal forest has been described as the "world's largest and most important carbon storehouse."[152] The 2010 study that provided data for **Figure 12** also estimated the carbon storage in the lands overlying the various resources (e.g., California oil, Alberta oil sands). The study estimated that the soil carbon ratio (tons of carbon per hectare) and biomass carbon ratio was approximately five and four times greater, respectively, in oil sands areas than in California oil sites.[153]

A further consideration is the fate of the land after the resources are extracted. In Alberta, an environmental law requires an oil sands development company to demonstrate that it has reclaimed the land to an "equivalent land capability."[154] Subsequent regulations have expanded on the meaning of this phrase:

> The ability of the land to support various land uses after conservation and reclamation is similar to the ability that existed prior to an activity being conducted on the land, but that the individual land uses will not necessarily be identical.[155]

The Alberta reclamation requirement is not unique. The United States has similar requirements that may apply in certain instances. For example, the Bureau of Land Management (BLM) has reclamation regulations that apply to oil and gas operations on federal lands.[156] BLM guidance states:

> The long-term objective of final reclamation is to set the course for eventual ecosystem restoration, including the restoration of the natural vegetation community, hydrology, and wildlife habitats. In most cases, this means returning the land to a condition approximating or equal to that which existed prior to the disturbance. The operator is generally not responsible for achieving full ecological restoration of the site.[157]

A comparison between the U.S. and Canadian reclamation requirements and their applications is beyond the scope of this report. However, data from Alberta indicate that reclamation has not kept pace with land disturbance. Data from 2010 indicate that approximately 8% of the total disturbed area has been permanently reclaimed.[158] Of the permanently reclaimed land, 2% has been

---

[152] Rebecca Rooney et al, "Oil Sands Mining and Reclamation Cause Massive Loss of Peatland and Stored Carbon," *Proceedings of the National Academy of Sciences*, 109: 4933-4937, 2012.

[153] Sonia Yeh et al, "Land Use Greenhouse Gas Emissions from Conventional Oil Production and Oil Sands," *Environmental Science and Technology*, 44(22): 8766-8722, 2010.

[154] Alberta Environmental Protection and Enhancement Act (as of November 2010), at http://www.qp.alberta.ca/documents/Acts/E12.pdf.

[155] Alberta Conservation and Reclamation Regulation, AR 115/93. For a discussion of this regulation and its applications, see P. Gosselin et al., *Environmental and Health Impacts of Canada's Oil Sands Industry*, The Royal Society of Canada, Expert Panel Report, Ottawa, Ontario, December 15, 2010.

[156] See e.g., 43 CFR Section 3101.1-2 and BLM Onshore Oil and Gas Lease Form (Form 3100-11), Section 12.

[157] United States Department of the Interior and Department of Agriculture, *Surface Operating Standards and Guidelines for Oil and Gas Exploration and Development*, ("Gold Book"), 2007, p. 43.

[158] The total disturbed area includes cleared areas, disturbed areas, and areas ready for reclamation. These categories are defined by the following source: Alberta Government, Oil Sands Mine Regional Totals for Reclamation and (continued...)

---

certified per Alberta requirements (equating with 0.16% of the total disturbed area). The 2010 Royal Society of Canada report stated:

> Because of the very small amount of land certified to date relative to the large area that has been disturbed in the oil sands region, there is major skepticism as to whether reclamation to an equivalent land capability can be achieved in a reasonable time frame.[159]

Subsequent to that report, a 2012 study from the Proceedings of the National Academy of Sciences assessed pre- and post-reclamation data at several oil sands mining sites. The study found that lost wetlands were not being replaced, resulting in a "dramatic loss of carbon storage and sequestration potential."[160]

Water Resources and Quality Issues

While the water resource impacts from oil sands development are seen by some stakeholders as largely a Canadian domestic issues, other stakeholders view the environmental consequences of oil sands development as part of the global discussion about the long-term implications of unconventional oil and gas. At issue is whether oil sands development may harm the water resources and aquatic ecosystems and species of the northern Alberta and the northern territories.

Both oil sands in situ and surface mining techniques have water resource impacts. In situ processes use groundwater that is brought to the surface and heated, then reinjected for the underground steam-based separation of the oil from the sand. Surface mining operations withdraw water from the north-flowing Athabasca River. This water is heated for use in the complex separation process of liberating the oil from the sands. Process wastestreams are collected in tailings ponds or lakes, which can cover a substantial area.

Mining also results in significant land disturbance which later requires remediation; how effective remediation is at long-term restoration and protection of water resources is a subject of on-going debate. Additionally, maintaining the mine site requires capturing and disposing of surface water and groundwater entering the site. The potential wetlands and associated migratory bird impacts from changes in surface water and groundwater regimes that result both from direct water use in-situ and mining operations and indirectly through long-term changes to the landscape also are concerns.

On a direct water use per unit of energy basis, the oil sands processes are comparable or below the intensity of U.S. onshore oil production using freshwater for enhanced oil recovery, and considerably below the water intensity of corn or soy biofuels.[161] Water use for oil sands,

---

(...continued)

Disturbance Tracking by Year, at http://environment.alberta.ca.

[159] P. Gosselin et al., *Environmental and Health Impacts of Canada's Oil Sands Industry*, The Royal Society of Canada, Expert Panel Report, Ottawa, Ontario, December 15, 2010, p. 194.

[160] Rebecca Rooney et al, "Oil Sands Mining and Reclamation Cause Massive Loss of Peatland and Stored Carbon," *Proceedings of the National Academy of Sciences*, 109: 4933-4937, 2012.

[161] Currently there is no authoritative source comparing the water intensities of a wide range of fuels on an energy basis. Water intensity data for shale oil and life-cycle water use for gas-to-liquids are particularly scarce. Existing data sources all have shortcomings; therefore, this paragraph is based on information compiled from a number of different sources, including C. King and M. Webber, "Water Intensity of Transportation," *Environmental Science & Technology*, vol. 42, no. 21 (2009), available at http://pubs.acs.org/doi/pdf/10.1021/es800367m; P. Gosselin et al., *Environmental* (continued...)

---

however, is likely to exceed the freshwater intensity of offshore and conventional oil production, which use processes that do not employ or require freshwater inputs for their development. The freshwater intensity of in-situ oil sands production is generally 17% to 25% percent of oil sands mining; however, while more water efficient, in-situ production leaves in place (i.e., unrecovered) a considerable portion of the petroleum resources. The current direct water efficiency of oil sands production may improve as new technologies are employed.

Much of the concern with oil sands development (and other types of unconventional oil and gas development) is the concentration of water use and impacts within a limited geographic area. One concern is that water use for oil sands mining reduces river flows, particularly during low flows periods. To manage these concerns, oil sands operators are required to obtain water withdrawal licenses, and a water management framework was developed to protect in-stream flows in the Athabasca River. The framework identifies how water withdrawals are to be reduced during low flow periods. A report by an expert panel of the Royal Society of Canada concluded that "water use at current levels does not threaten viability of the Athabasca River system if the Water Management Framework...is fully implemented and enforced."[162] Another concern is groundwater depletion. The expert panel report found that "there needs to be greater attention directed to regional groundwater resources" which currently are not well characterized, and that there was no evidence of a framework to limit groundwater extraction.[163]

In addition, water quality monitoring data have generated some debate. A 2012 study found that the oil sands operations "substantially increases the loadings of toxic PPE [priority pollutant elements] to the Athabasca River and its tributaries."[164] Moreover, seven PPE— cadmium, copper, lead, mercury, nickel, silver, and zinc—exceeded Canada or Alberta guidelines for aquatic life protection. The authors pointed out that their study contradicted results from the Regional Aquatic Monitoring Program (RAMP).[165] For example, the 2011 RAMP Technical Report stated that "differences in water quality measured in fall 2011 between all test and one of the upper baseline stations in the Athabasca River were classified as Negligible-Low compared to the regional baseline conditions."[166]

RAMP describes itself as "an industry-funded, multi-stakeholder environmental monitoring program" that began in 1997. RAMP results are often highlighted as evidence of the minimal impacts to water resources due to oil sands development.[167]

(...continued)

and Health Impacts of Canada's Oil Sands Industry, The Royal Society of Canada, Expert Panel Report, Ottawa, Ontario, December 15, 2010, p. 51.
http://www.rsc.ca/documents/expert/RSC%20report%20complete%20secured%209Mb.pdf; DOE, *Energy Demands on Water Resources Report to Congress on the Interdependency of Energy and Water*, Dec. 2006; Canadian Association of Petroleum Producers, *Water Use in Canada's Oil Sands*, July 2011.

[162] P. Gosselin et al., *Environmental and Health Impacts of Canada's Oil Sands Industry*, The Royal Society of Canada, Expert Panel Report, Ottawa, Ontario, December 15, 2010, p. 284.

[163] Ibid., p. 285.

[164] Erin Kelly et al, "Oil Sands Development Contributes Elements Toxic at Low Concentrations to the Athabasca River and Its Tributaries," *Proceedings of the National Academy of Sciences*, 107: 16178-16183, 2010.

[165] See annual Technical Reports and Community Reports, at http://www.ramp-alberta.org.

[166] RAMP, 2011 Technical Report, Executive Summary, at http://www.ramp-alberta.org/UserFiles/File/RAMP_2011_Final_Executive_Summary.pdf.

[167] See e.g., Government of Alberta, Oil Sands Factsheet: Protecting the Environment, at http://www.oilsands.alberta.ca/FactSheets/Protecting_the_Environment%283%29.pdf.

Appendix. Additional Information

Table A-1. Agencies With Jurisdiction or Expertise Relevant to Pipeline Impacts
Not Including Department of State

Agency	Role/Responsibilities in the Keystone XL Pipeline
EPA	Oversees state-implemented permit programs administered pursuant to the Section 402 of the Clean Water Act (CWA) regarding National Pollutant Discharge Elimination System (NPDES). The NPDES program covers point-source discharges of pollutants into U.S. waters. In addition, EPA reviews and comments on U.S. Army Corps of Engineers permit applications (per CWA Section 404).
U.S. Army Corps of Engineers (Corps)	Issues permits for sections of the pipeline that require placement of dredge and fill material in waters of the United States, including wetlands (pursuant CWA Section 404), or for pipeline crossings of navigable waters (pursuant to Section 10 of the Rivers and Harbors Act);
Department of the Interior (DOI)	The Bureau of Land Management (BLM) is authorized to grant temporary use permits for portions of the project that would encroach on federal lands.
	The National Park Service (NPS) is responsible for providing technical review of the proposal in the vicinity of NPS-administered lands affected by the proposed Project.
	The U.S. Fish and Wildlife Service is responsible for ensuring project compliance with the Endangered Species Act and would provide a Biological Opinion if the project is likely to adversely affect federally listed species.
U.S. Department of Agriculture (USDA)	The Natural Resources Conservation Service (NRCS) administers the Wetlands Reserve Program under which it purchases conservation easements and provides cost share to landowners for the purposes of restoring and protecting wetlands.
Department of Transportation (DOT)	The Pipeline and Hazardous Materials Safety Administration (PHMSA), Office of Pipeline Safety (OPS) has the safety-related authority for the nation's natural gas and hazardous liquid pipelines. PHMSA evaluates risks; develops and enforces standards for design, construction, operations and maintenance of pipelines; responds to accidents/incidents; conducts research on promising technologies; provides grants to states to support their pipeline safety programs; and reviews oil spill response plans.
U.S. Department of Energy (DOE)	The Office of Policy and International Affairs (PI) provides advice to DOE on existing and prospective energy-related policies. At the request of DOS, PI provided assistance in the analysis of the proposed project in light of world crude oil market demand, and domestic and global energy challenges ranging from energy price and market volatility to the long-term technology transitions related to greenhouse gas emissions reduction, energy efficiency, and the use of renewable resources.
	The Western Area Power Administration (Western) is a federal power-marketing agency that sells and delivers federal electric power to municipalities, public utilities, federal and state agencies, and Native American tribes in 15 western and central states. Western consulted with DOS to ensure cultural resources potentially affected by any Western transmission lines are taken into account.
Montana Department of Environmental Quality (MDEQ)	Keystone is required to obtain a Certificate of Compliance from MDEQ under the Montana Major Facility Siting Act (MFSA) before the proposed project may begin construction or acquire easements in Montana through the eminent domain process.
Various state/county agencies	Various agencies must consult on and/or consider issuing permits for projects that cross navigable waters or state highways, or involve work potentially affecting state streams, cultural resources, or natural resources.

Source: CRS, based on a review of the U.S. Department of State's, *Final Environmental Impact Statement for the Proposed Keystone XL Project: Introduction*, amended September 2011, p. 1-12 to p.1-17.

Figure A-1. Alternate Route Near the Nebraska Sandhills

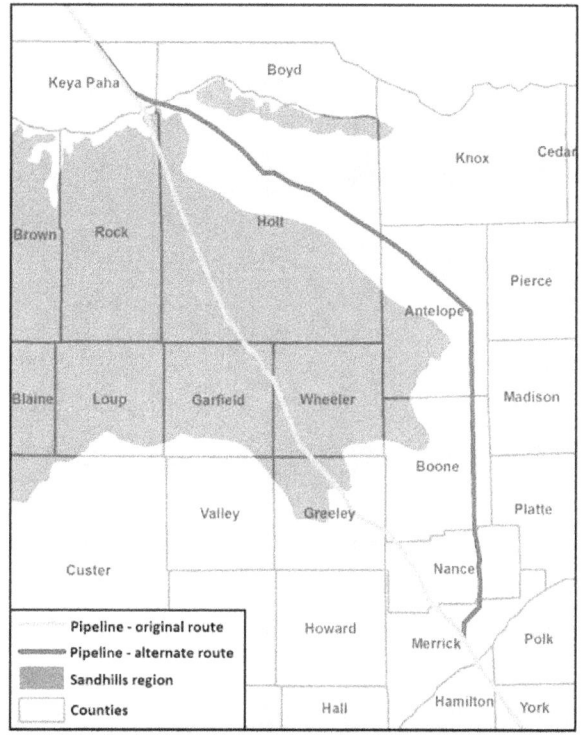

Source: Congressional Research Service, adapted from TransCanada, *TransCanada Keystone XL Pipeline Project, Initial Report Identifying Alternative and Preferred Corridors for Nebraska Reroute*, April 18, 2012, http://www.eenews.net/assets/2012/04/19/document_cw_02.pdf.

Author Contact Information

Jonathan L. Ramseur, Coordinator
Specialist in Environmental Policy
jramseur@crs.loc.gov, 7-7919

Richard K. Lattanzio
Analyst in Environmental Policy
rlattanzio@crs.loc.gov, 7-1754

Linda Luther
Analyst in Environmental Policy
lluther@crs.loc.gov, 7-6852

Paul W. Parfomak
Specialist in Energy and Infrastructure Policy
pparfomak@crs.loc.gov, 7-0030

Nicole T. Carter
Specialist in Natural Resources Policy
ncarter@crs.loc.gov, 7-0854